P9-AGQ-259

PERSONAL CHEF
*Marketing*
*Recipes for Success.*

# Become a Personal Chef

## 2004 Edition

## An Introduction to the Industry

# Brian T. Koning

641
.5023
KONING
2004

Library Resource Center
Renton Technical College
3000 N.E. 4th St.
Renton WA 98056

While every precaution has been taken in the preparation of this product, the author assumes no responsibility for errors or omissions, or for damages resulting from the use of the information contained herein. This book is sold with the understanding that the author and publisher are not engaged in rendering financial, legal and professional advice. Laws and practices vary from state to state and if any legal or other expert assistance is required, the services of a professional should be sought.

Copyright ©2004 by Brian T. Koning  All rights reserved.

No part of this publication may be reproduced, stored in a retrieval system, or transmitted in any form or by any means, electronic, mechanical, photocopying, recording or otherwise, without the prior permission of the copyright owner.

While the contents of this book are based on fact, certain events or examples have been fictionalized or embelished for educational content and impact.

First published by AuthorHouse 05/04/04

ISBN: 1-4184-0898-0 (e-book)
ISBN: 1-4184-0895-6 (Paperback)

Library of Congress Control Number: 2004091310

This book is printed on acid free paper.

Printed in the United States of America
Bloomington, IN

All Trademarks are recognized as belonging to their respective companies.

are Trademarks of
DOCTOR DINNER, LLC.

Library Resource Center
Renton Technical College
3000 N.E. 4th St.
Renton, WA 98056

# Acknowledgements

I first want to thank Doreen, my wife, and Kaitlin, Karli and Kyler, my children, for being as patient with me as possible while I was researching and writing this book. The long telephone calls, late nights, early mornings, countless hours on the computer and lack of attentiveness are the unfortunate by-products of the writing process. I love you.

I want to recognize my Grandma and Grandpa Koning and Grandma and Grandpa Schilling, although they are no longer with us, for fostering my love of food and cooking when I was very young.

To my parents, Bob and DeEtta Koning for teaching me the basics of cooking and for encouraging me to try everything on my plate, "Thank You." And to my sister, Alicia, who always provides support and encouragement for everything I do; I hope you are as proud of me as I am of you.

I want to thank personal chef Doug Gifford of Chef Caesars Cuisine, a friend and fellow thespian, for introducing me to the personal chef industry.

There are also countless contributors to this book. Most importantly, I want to acknowledge and thank the pioneers and industry leaders including David and Susan MacKay (USPCA), Candy Wallace (APCA), and Sharon Worster and Wendy Perry (both of the PCN). I appreciate your input to this book and recognize your hard work and dedication to the personal chef industry. There are many personal chefs, too many to single out, that have also contributed to this book either by offering their advice or reviewing the initial drafts. Thank you.

I want to thank my clients who have given me the opportunity to grow as a personal chef.

And finally, I want to thank God. He has helped me to close doors that led to empty promises while opening others leading to some pretty amazing adventures and experiences.

*-Brian*

# Contents

**Foreword**

In one of my favorite movies of all time, "Field of Dreams," Iowa farmer Ray Kinsella hears a voice in his cornfield tell him, "If you build it, they will come." He interprets this message as an instruction to build a baseball field on his farm, upon which appear the ghosts of Shoeless Joe Jackson and the other seven Chicago White Sox players banned from the game for throwing the 1919 World Series. When the voices continue, Ray, played by actor Kevin Costner, seeks out a reclusive author to help him understand the meaning of the messages and the purpose for his field.

I believe this movie symbolizes the way many people, myself included, have entered the personal chef industry. There was a nagging voice inside telling us to build it.

In the movie, Ray razed the land, planted grass, hauled in sand, built the bleachers, lined the base paths and even wired the stadium lights all by himself. Those around him watched from a distance while scratching their head and waiting for him to fail. In the end, a massive caravan of cars inched its way down the country road as people flocked from all over to see the game at Ray's new field.

Perhaps it was that same little voice appearing out of nowhere telling you, "Build a personal chef business and people will come running to you, salivating and begging you to make their life easier and healthier."

You're contemplating changing your career and life as you now know it. Listen to your inner voice and learn to ignore the voices of friends, family and co-workers around you muttering, "I hope you know what you're doing."

I've been there. In fact, I'm still there. Here I am with just three years' experience as a personal chef, writing a book that I hope someone will buy. My little voice kept saying, "Write it and they will read it and take all of your advice and become a successful personal chef." Like Ray, who gave up cash crops of corn to build a baseball diamond, I've traded part of my income from my personal chef business to sit down at my computer eight to twelve hours a day for the past few months to finish this book.

And, I know there are people questioning why I am spending time writing this book. They are just waiting for me to fail so they can say, "I told you so!"

If you ask any of the other 6,000 or so personal chefs that are cultivating their businesses, they've been where you are. In fact, some of the more experienced personal chefs will tell you that they have actually started over several times. Changes in the economy, client turnover, diet fads, burnout, and other factors may, and probably will, require you to jump-start your business periodically. I've had to do it.

Ray listened to those voices, followed his dreams and built his field. So did I. And so have people like Susan and David MacKay, Candy Wallace, Sharon Worster and Wendy Perry. And there are others like Douglas Gifford, Tom Baletti, Lisa Dillard, Lynch Orr, Cindi Billington, Laura Cotton and thousands more.

But, this is not Hollywood. This is real life. If you build it, they might come. But, it takes work. It takes compassion and know-how. It takes personality and resolve. It takes gritting your teeth and being able to suck it up when the going gets tough. It takes a sense of humor, humility and the ability to admit mistakes. Most of all, it takes time.

*"It takes twenty years to become an overnight success."*

— Eddie Cantor

*"The elevator to success is out of order. You'll have to use the stairs... one step at a time."*

— Joe Girard

# Introduction

If you are looking for all of the answers to building and running a personal  chef business in this book, you aren't going to find them. This book is only intended to help give you a perspective on a relatively new and emerging industry. If you are contemplating becoming a personal chef or are a relatively new personal chef struggling to get your business to take flight, this book is for you.

The sagging economy, the recent rise in unemployment and the waning confidence that people have in their job security are all factors that are influencing people to look at new careers. The personal chef industry has received a lot of press lately. *Entrepreneur Magazine* recently chose it as fourth best home-based business to start in 2004.

I became a personal chef for a variety of reasons. After spending 18 years fluttering from job to job in sales, marketing and advertising, I was tired of the corporate bureaucracy. I was also concerned about being able to find any job stability in the midst of a sputtering economy. After getting downsized in 2000, I decided it was time to make a career change.

My good friend Douglas Gifford, of Chef Caesars Cuisine in Indianapolis, introduced me to the personal chef industry back in the Fall of 2000. Doug and I met while performing in a community theater production.  When he learned that we shared a love of cooking and enjoyed preparing food for cast parties, he told me that he was a personal chef. He gave me a video about the personal chef industry. I watched it and was hooked.

For the next several months, I researched the industry extensively. I read every Internet article I could find. I researched all of the personal chef associations. And, I even called and talked to several other personal chefs from across the country. Because I had a strong background in business, marketing, and advertising and I knew my way around the kitchen, I believed I could be successful as a personal chef. I joined the United States Personal Chef Association and opened my business on February 12, of 2001.

I immediately sent out a press release to friends, family, and the local media. Success came quickly — almost too quickly. Less than a week later, I cooked for my first client. Over the next two weeks, I made my first television appearance  on Indianapolis' ABC affiliate, doing a segment on healthy cooking; and I was featured in a large article on the front page of a local newspaper. The calls and E-mail were flooding in.

When I first joined the United States Personal Chef Association, I jumped right in and started participating in the online forums. I read many postings from other members who had been struggling for months, or even a couple of years, to build a client base and generate a respectable income. I was ecstatic to be at capacity within 45 days.

It was so easy for me. Why were other personal chefs, some with years of experience, struggling? And, I questioned why anyone would start a personal chef business when they lacked the business and marketing skills needed to be successful. I figured that if I could find answers to those questions, and more, I would be able to help other aspiring personal chefs determine if this was, indeed, a viable venture. That's why I wrote this book.

I don't want to mislead you and make you think that you can go out tomorrow, next week, next month or even six months from now and start turning a profit. I also don't want to discourage you from following your dreams.

Take my advice and the advice of others for what its worth. More importantly, make use of the resources in this book and follow your heart.

Good luck!

# Chapter 1

# *The New Culinary Career*

## Defining "Chef"

Before I offer my definition of what I believe a personal chef is, we need define the term "chef." A "chef" is the person (or persons) in charge of overseeing cooking operations in a kitchen.

## Getting "Personal"

A person who provides a business service in which he or she goes into a client's home and cooks a number of meals that the client will consume over the next week, two weeks or month is, by definition, a "Personal Chef." But, the definition of a personal chef does not stop here. A personal chef is also a business owner responsible for overseeing all aspects of his or her business from simple accounting procedures, advertising, and selling to menu planning, shopping, cooking and, yes, even crisis management.

Most personal chefs cook for five to ten different clients every two to four weeks. Clients can range from single people, single parents or middle- and high-income families to empty nesters, the elderly and the sick.

Most of my clients are just normal folks who want to eat healthy and are sick and tired of fast food, pizza and spending three hours a night in a noisy restaurant.

Now, back to the definition of a chef. In layman's terms, a chef is the person in charge of running a kitchen. I point this out because personal chefs have received a lot of criticism in the past. And, until just a few years ago, this booming industry has been ignored as a viable culinary career. I found that the majority of those who rebuff the personal chef designation are involved in culinary studies or have attended culinary schools or training programs.

Although I, like more than 60 percent of the active personal chefs, am a self-taught cook, I do provide personal cooking services in a client's home. Because I am in charge of overseeing those cooking activities, I am, by definition, a personal chef. Enough said.

## Defending the Profession to Trained Chefs

I recently crossed paths with a professionally trained chef that graduated from the prestigious Johnson and Wales culinary program. She questioned how I could claim to be a "chef" when I had not attended, let alone graduated from, a recognized culinary program. I simply told her that I was "a culinary prodigy." Needless to say, she didn't like that tongue-in-cheek answer very much. She spent tens of thousands of dollars on her culinary education. But, I have also completed my college education and invested a lot of time and resources learning how to cook; just not through a culinary program.

For some, becoming a personal chef is no different than the basketball player who decides to enter the NBA right out of high school or the child who performs a piano concerto at Carnegie Hall without completing even one college music course.  If you possess the skills, talent and desire to fulfill your dreams, go for it.

## Private Chef Versus Personal Chef

Some people confuse personal chefs with private chefs. Private chefs usually cook for one client while personal chefs cook for multiple clients. Also, a private chef is usually paid an annual salary by that person that could reach into the $100,000 range. Personal chef services are very affordable for most families; it's comparable to eating out at a family restaurant.

Who would hire a private chef? Famous people like Oprah Winfrey have private chefs that prepare fresh meals for them throughout the day. A private chef may cook for a politician, a touring rock & roll band, an actor, an athlete, or other wealthy individuals. A private chef is usually well compensated but puts in a lot of hours and generally has no other life outside of cooking for the rich and famous. Private chefs must be accessible nearly 24/7 and be able to travel as needed.

# Chapter 2

# *In the Beginning*

The earliest reference to a personal chef I can find dates back to 1671 in which a story makes mention of the "personal chef" to the Duke of Plessis-Praslin in France. The story goes that, as with many kitchen mishaps, this personal chef wasn't paying close attention to what he was doing and a pan full of burnt sugar boiled over, spilling onto a pile of almonds. The curious Duke took one taste and loved it. He named the new confection after himself; hence, "praslin" then became "praline". Pralines were later perfected by Belgian chocolatiers.

## Organizing A New Industry

Personal chefs have existed in North America in some form or another ever since the Pilgrims landed at Plymouth Rock. Settlers would cook for other settlers in exchange for services such as blacksmithing, carpentering, dressmaking and more.

Present day, the founders of the United States Personal Chef Association get the credit for actually launching the personal chef industry on a national level. Susan and David MacKay started "Personally Yours" personal chef service in San Diego, California in 1988. Together, they were responsible for organizing the first group of personal chefs and founded the USPCA in 1992.

The MacKays then established the United States Personal Chef Institute (now the Culinary Business Academy) in 1996 to provide a comprehensive training curriculum. The USPCA hosted the first national Personal Chef conference in 1997 and awarded its new Certified Personal Chef (CPC) designation to 15 of the attendees. Today, the Culinary Business Academy continues to provide comprehensive training and the USPCA offers support while trying to standardize a somewhat fragmented industry.

While the MacKay's and the USPCA launched the personal chef movement, it was only natural that others would follow and competition would emerge.

## Other Associations Follow

As the industry began to grow, other personal chefs formed their own associations. In the mid-1990s, Candy Wallace left behind a 20-year career in corporate sales and marketing and started "The Serving Spoon" personal chef service in San Diego, California. In 1996, she co-found the San Diego County Association of Personal Chefs. Wallace, along with then business partner Denise Monroy, decided to expand the association regionally by forming the Personal Chef Association.

The PCA was the precursor to Wallace's national personal chef training venture, the American Personal Chef Institute (APCI) and the American Personal Chef Association that Wallace founded in 1996. Since founding the APCA and APCI, Wallace has continued to focus much of her efforts on getting the culinary industry to recognize the Personal Chef profession as a legitimate career path.

After a six-year effort by Wallace, the American Culinary Federation now offers two personal chef certification levels. These certifications can be pursued and attained by any personal chef, regardless of their association affiliation.

Sharon Worster, a former physician's nurse and Wendy Perry, a former cooking instructor, co-found the Personal Chefs Network in February of 2000. Their mission was to provide a more intimate networking and support environment for personal chefs while providing benefits and services that filled a niche not covered by the other associations. Although Worster resides in Texas and Perry lives in North Carolina, the Internet allows them to effectively manage their association and be readily accessible to PCN members.

Today, all three associations continue to make strides to advance the plight of personal chefs. You can visit their web site and view each association's list of accomplishments.

## Industry Statistics and Trends

Trying to get a handle on the current state of the Personal Chef industry is tricky due to a lack of verifiable statistics. According to a variety of unconfirmed sources, the personal chef industry claims that there are anywhere from 7,000 to 10,000 personal chef services actively operating in the United States. These personal chefs are said to be serving between 80,000 to 100,000 families.

The problem is, these are the same figures that the industry was reporting as far back as 1999. There were also predictions then that 25,000 personal chefs would be serving some 300,000 families by 2004. That hasn't happened.

Truth be told, there is no scientific method for counting the current number of personal chef businesses or accurately predicting future trends.

My own conservative estimate of the number of practicing personal chefs is approximately 6,000 and serving 60,000 to 90,000 families.

Here's how I arrived at my estimate. The USPCA and the PCN report active, verifiable memberships of 2,376 and 600 respectively. That accounts for 3,000.

The American Personal Chef Association, according to Executive Director Candy Wallace, does not audit its membership numbers. However, if the percentage of APCA members that list their business with the association's online personal chef locator is consistent with that of the other two associations, that would put the current APCA active membership at approximately 1,500 (± 300).

I combined the estimated 4,500 associations' members along with the estimated number of personal chefs that have not joined an association or belong to multiple associations. Even figuring in an error ratio of plus or minus 500, it would be a stretch to find 6,000 personal chef businesses actively operating today. However, that's the number I'm going to go with unless anyone else can come up with verifiable proof that the count is higher or lower.

The number of people entering the profession is growing, but probably not as rapidly as industry leaders project. And, there are people leaving the industry due to lack of success. But, even if the total number of personal chefs doubles over the next five years, it is undoubtedly one of the fastest growing culinary professions. Several colleges, universities and accredited culinary programs are finally recognizing the personal chef is a legitimate career path and they are now offering students enrolled in the culinary arts the opportunity to specialize in personal chef studies.

# Potential Earnings

So, how much money can you earn as a personal chef? Again, that's up to interpretation and can get just a bit confusing. So, try to hang with me here.

The statistics being reported by some of the associations don't add up. If, as reported, this is a $200 million dollar industry and there are 10,000 personal chefs serving 100,000 families, that means the average client spends about $2,000 per year. If there are 10,000 (an industry estimate) personal chefs, each one would be serving an average of 10 clients per year. According to those numbers, you could expect to gross approximately $20,000. With a net profit of even 60 percent, you are only looking at net earnings of $12,000. Welcome to poverty!

If you take my estimate of 6,000 personal chefs, each one cooking for 15 clients each month and grossing $350 on average, the numbers start to look a little more attractive. That's about $63,000 per year gross income. At a 50% profit, that's $31,500 net income. That would make this a $400 million industry.

A recent survey conducted by the USPCA reveals that approximately 63 percent of all personal chefs operate their business on a part time basis. Average that number, and there are approximately 4,000 personal chefs grossing about $40,000 part time. Depending on how thrifty of a shopper you are and by keeping your expenses at a minimum, you could easily net $25,000 a year.

If this is, indeed, a $400 million industry and 4,000 personal chefs account for $160 million, then the remaining 2,000 account for the $240 million in gross revenue. That calculates out to an average of $120,000 per personal chef, or an approximate net profit of about $70,000; a respectable income for an independent, full time business

## You Do the Math

If you set your goal at netting even $150 per day cooking four days a week, you will earn $30,000. With a little help from your accountant, you can greatly reduce your tax liability and keep a large percentage of your gross income. This is easily obtainable only working part-time. With a little effort and the right client mix, you can net $250 per day. Even working just four days per week, you can gross about $50,000. Now, were cooking!

If you need to meet a financial goal or replace a lost income, follow this formula to determine how many clients you need to cook for on a weekly basis for 50 weeks (take some time off for vacation).

Desired Gross Income _____

Divided by 50 _____ = Weekly Gross

Divide the Weekly Gross by $200 (targeted net profit)

Equals _____ Clients Per Week

For example, let's say you were recently downsized or left a job where you made $42,000 per year. You would need to clear $840 per week. If you set your sites on earning a net profit of $200 per cook day, you would need to cook for four clients per week and pick up an occasional cook day or special event every couple of weeks.

## Other Income Sources

There are many other cooking arrangements or add-on services that you can provide to help you meet your financial goals. I'll discuss those opportunities in greater detail in Chapter 16. I truly believe that if you work your business full time, have a good marketing plan in place and focus your attention on cooking for families, instead of individuals or couples, you can easily make $60-$75,000. That's as much as a lot of executive chefs make working ten to fourteen hours a day, including weekends, sweating over a stove in a crowded, stressful commercial kitchen. Not my cup of tea!

## Client Turnover

Just know that your client list will change and your business will go through periods of growth as well as slumps. You'll have clients that will stay with you for years while you will have some clients that you only cook for once. My business slows down in late July through mid-August because of vacations. But when the school year starts, business booms again.

You need to plan for the down times and fill that time with prospecting and lead generation activities. And, you need to take a break. You can experience burnout, just like with any other profession.

Library Resource Center
Renton Technical College
3000 N.E. 4th St.
Renton, WA  98056

12

Library Resource Center
Renton Technical College
3000 N E. 4th St.
Renton, WA 98056

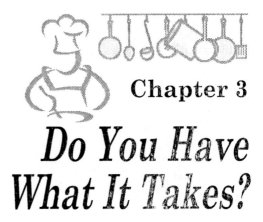

## Chapter 3

# *Do You Have What It Takes?*

Now that you know a little bit about the history of the personal chef industry, its current status and where it appears to be heading, it's time to evaluate just how ready you are to launch your career as a personal chef.

The general rule in almost any industry, business, or sales job is that 80 percent of the business is going to be generated by 20 percent of the people doing the work. This means that you must be equipped with the necessary skills to put yourself in the position to be in the upper echelon of the personal chef industry.

Being a personal chef is not for everyone. I recently helped an acquaintance get started in the business after he was downsized from a job in the computer technology industry. He has the culinary skills. But, he admittedly lacks the marketing and sales skills. I view myself to be a reasonably successful personal chef and don't mind helping others get started—

hence, this book. It took him about seven weeks to sigh his first clients. I invited him to shadow me on one of my cook day where we had the opportunity to discuss several marketing issues and he was able to see what an actual cook day was like. We discussed the need to put a plan in place and, while it is important to stay focused, not to get too technical or caught up in minute details.

Deciding to be a personal chef is a major decision that is not to be taken lightly. You will not be successful if you are disorganized, prone to procrastinate or unwilling to learn from others who are successful. It's also not to be taken too seriously. Have fun and develop a sense of humor. If you are too serious, you will burn out.

Before you read any further, complete this brief survey to determine if you have the basic skills needed to launch your personal chef business. This survey is not scientific. But, I believe it will allow you to evaluate your knowledge about cooking, business, marketing and sales. For each statement, give yourself a score of "0" if you are "Not Confident", a "1" if you are "Somewhat Confident", or a "2" if you are "Very Confident". Be honest.

## Personal Chef Confidence Survey

### Section A: Cooking

I consider myself to be a competent cook.    _____

My friends and family like my cooking.    _____

I can read a recipe and make necessary adjustments.    _____

I am familiar with most cooking terminology.    _____

I am familiar with kitchen utensils and their use.    _____

I am familiar with various types of cook tops & ranges.    _____

I know the characteristics of most herbs and spices.    _____

I know the difference between knives and their use.    _____

I can convert units of measurement.    _____

I know the difference between baking and roasting. 		_____

I can explain the different methods of cooking. 		_____

I know what proteins and carbohydrates are. 		_____

I know the various ways to cook poultry. 		_____

I know the various ways to cook fish and seafood. 		_____

I know how to prepare various cuts of beef and pork. 		_____

I know how to prepare and cook fresh vegetables. 		_____

I know what "mire poix's" or "holy trinity" is. 		_____

I know how to prepare sauces and gravies. 		_____

I know how to cook rice and pasta. 		_____

I am familiar with food handling and safety. 		_____

**Total Section A** 		_____

## Section B: Business

I know what a Sole Proprietorship is. 		_____

I know the difference between an LLC and S Corp. 		_____

I know how to check business name availability. 		_____

I know what licensing is required for my business. 		_____

I know the tax benefits of various business entities. 		_____

I understand basic accounting principles. 		_____

I am a good record keeper. 		_____

I know how to write a business plan. 		_____

I know where to turn for small business support. 		_____

I have established a business banking relationship. 		_____

I have access to a computer and the Internet. 		_____

I have a resource for business forms and contracts. 		_____

I plan to accept credit cards as a form of payment. 		_____

I know where to get insurance for my business. 		_____

I can live off of my savings for at least six months. 		_____

**Total Section B** 		_____

## Section C: Marketing and Advertising

I know how to prepare a marketing plan. _____

I know where to turn for marketing support. _____

I possess solid writing skills. _____

I am able to speak in front of large groups. _____

I have solid presentation skills. _____

I have a resource for marketing/sales collateral. _____

I am familiar with my city's demographics. _____

I know how to write and distribute a press release. _____

I am not afraid to tell strangers about my business. _____

I take pride in my professional appearance. _____

I am capable of aggressively promoting my business. _____

I know how to get "free" publicity. _____

I know how to network with other businesses. _____

I plan on having an Internet web site for my business. _____

I know how to use the Internet as a marketing tool. _____

**Total Section C** _____


## Section D: Sales & Customer Service

I know where to find prospective clients. _____

I know how to pre-qualify and qualify prospects. _____

I am confident talking on the telephone. _____

I know how to put together a sales presentation. _____

I make a good first impression. _____

I have strong presentation skills. _____

I am a good listener. _____

I am a good note taker. _____

I put people at ease. _____

I can admit it when I don't know the answer. _____

During a sales call, I can ask for client's business.          _____

I know at least 3 methods of countering objections.          _____

I am comfortable asking for feedback.          _____

I am open to client feedback and criticism.          _____

I can remain calm under pressure.          _____

**Total Section D**          _____


Section A Total          _____

Section B Total          _____

Section C Total          _____

Section D Total          _____

**Total Score**          _____


| Score | Recommendation |
|---|---|
| [120-130] | Go for it! You could be a successful Personal Chef. |
| [100-119] | You have a good foundation. Do more research. |
| [80 - 99] | You need to develop skills in deficient areas. |
| [65-79] | You need more formal training before moving on. |
| [Under 64] | The odds are against your success. |

So, how did you score? If I had taken this survey (which I developed for this book) when I first started, I would have scored 114. I needed to improve my culinary skills and knowledge about food safety. Whatever your score, please read on. Don't be over confident or too discouraged. The rest of this book goes into more of the specifics that will give you insight to what setting up your business entails; where to find help; and what it's really like to run a personal chef business.

## Shadow A Personal Chef

Lisa Dillard and Tom Baletti both operate their own personal chef businesses in San Antonio, Texas. When I met with them to discuss ideas for this book, they stressed the importance of marketing and business knowledge. Lisa, however stressed the point that you need to shadow one or more personal chefs in your area. This means that you contact them and get permission to ride along with them for a day or two. Lisa and Tom said that they almost always allow aspiring personal chefs to shadow then. Be ready to be put to work, however.

When you shadow a personal chef, you should:

- help plan a menu
- make out a shopping list
- shop for groceries
- prepare the kitchen
- assist with cooking
- assist with cooling, packaging and labeling
- assist with cleaning

If a personal chef agrees to let you shadow them, respect the fact that they are working. Prepare a list of questions, take notes, and do what you are told. Don't just sit there and chat. At the end of the shadowing session, or on another day, meet with your mentor to go over your notes and ask questions. Shadowing a personal chef will give you a good perspective about what your typical day will be like.

If there aren't any personal chefs in your area or you can't find one willing to help you, plan a road trip. You should be able to find a personal chef within a few hour's drive. You might have to spend the night at a hotel, but may be able to deduct travel, lodging and meals from your taxes.

## Chapter 4

# *Investing In Your New Venture*

Starting your own personal chef business is one of the most affordable businesses to start if you are resourceful. It can be very inexpensive (less than $500) to moderately expensive ($5,000). Cooking equipment, business fees, supplies, clothing, training materials, cooking classes and membership in professional associations all add up. On top of that, add marketing and advertising costs and you can quickly deplete your cash reserves or max out your credit cards very quickly.

## Initial Startup Costs

My startup costs totaled less than $500. I know other personal chefs who have invested nearly $25,000 before cooking for their first client. If you lack certain skills and need to take a few cooking, business or marketing classes, that's fine. Education is a wise and valid investment. But, purchasing a brand new minivan and having your logo painted on it is a bad investment.

I am an enigma in that my quick success was an exception rather than a rule. I have a lot of business experience and possess the ability to be resourceful enough to minimize my investment.

Here is an approximate itemization of my expenditures before cooking for my first client:

| | | |
|---|---|---|
| Association Membership | $250* | |
| Cookware & Knives | $0 | (used my own) |
| Cooking Utensils | $5 | (Dollar Store) |
| Clothing | $50 | (Aprons, Shoes, Chef's Hat) |
| Spices & Oils | $65 | (Discount Store) |
| Business Cards | $10 | (Printed My Own) |
| Flyers | $5 | (Printed My Own) |
| Plastic Tubs (for supplies) | $20 | (Walmart) |
| LLC Filing Fee | $90 | (Indiana) |
| Web site | $20 | (Yahoo!) |
| **Total** | **$495** | |

**\* USPCA membership did not require purchase of materials when I joined.**

Once you make your initial investment, land a few clients and get some cook dates under your belt, you can start purchasing new equipment and increase your advertising. I have since purchased new knives, cookware, storage equipment, chef wear and more.

## Calculate Your Startup Costs

Enter $0 if you don't need to purchase items.

| | |
|---|---|
| Association Membership | _____ |
| Business Filing Fees | _____ |
| Cookware | _____ |
| Knives | _____ |
| Utensils | _____ |
| Clothing | _____ |
| Towels | _____ |
| Spices & Oils | _____ |
| Business Cards | _____ |
| Flyers | _____ |
| Web site | _____ |
| **Total** | _____ |

## *Rich or Poor, It's Your Choice*

I believe that you need a personal plan as well as a business plan if you are going to own and operate your own business. You have three choices; build wealth, live from paycheck to paycheck, or go bankrupt. There is a fourth choice that involves soup kitchens and cold park benches – but we won't go there.  Your personal life is a business and should take priority. I speak from experience. Do not risk your personal success by gambling on business success.

There are some great books available on building wealth.  I encourage you to read the story of Arkad and his friends in *The Richest Man in Babylon* by George Clason. Learn and implement his rules of building wealth. It's a short book that, because it's written in a Biblical literary style, takes some thought and interpretation on your part.  I also recommend that you follow up with *Rich Dad, Poor Dad* by Robert T. Kiyosaki and Sharon L. Lechter. It's an easy read and puts the principles from Clason's book into the present day.

I recently had the opportunity to work as a part of a seminar team led by author, motivational speaker and bankruptcy expert, Stephen Snyder. In 2003, an estimated 1.6 million people declared bankruptcy. What I learned from Stephen was invaluable. I was sitting in a training session watching his seminar for the very first time. Paraphrasing what he communicated, also supported by the books I mention above, is this:

> *The only thing that separates the rich from the middle class is a simple change of your financial strategy. Simply put, those who live from paycheck to paycheck do so because they pay all of their bills and then save whatever is left over; which is usually nothing. The rich, however, pay themselves first and then pay their bills with whatever is left over.*

It was an epiphany, a financial sucker punch. In my fortieth year on this planet, I finally got it. Now, for every dollar I earn,

I put 10 percent into savings and another 10 percent toward my church. This still leaves 80 percent to pay my bills. That 10 percent I put into savings is untouchable unless it can be put toward an investment with a 100% guarantee of return. That doesn't mean investing in some "get rich quick" scheme. Just read the books and you'll understand.

If I have a few dollars left over after paying my bills, only then do I buy my $4.00 mocha latte or go to a first-run showing of a movie at the local cinema instead of waiting for it to come out on DVD.

Since adopting this strategy, I have transformed from an impulse spender to somewhat of a penny pincher. As I see my cash reserves and investments grow, I think twice before purchasing anything. I always shop around for the bargains and enjoy going garage sales, auctions, and thrift stores.

As a personal chef, you will have times when money rains down from above and times of financial drought. You need to pace your spending and set some money aside. When, business slows and the money isn't rolling in, use your time wisely by increasing your marketing activities.

A final piece of financial advice, treat your business with financial care – especially in the startup phase. If you spend money you don't have on new equipment, fancy chef's clothes, and a new van with your logo painted on the side, you are going to struggle to make a profit unless, of course, you already have the money to spare. Remember to crawl, walk, and then run.

## Chapter 5

# *Forming Your Business*

You need to determine what type of business entity you are going to create. There are three forms of business types that most personal chefs fall under. You could be a sole proprietorship, a "C" or "S" Corporation, a Limited Liability Company or other entity offered in your state. I'll give you a very basic overview of the different types of business entities in layman's terms. But, I strongly recommend visiting your State government's web site or contacting your Secretary of State's office for more information on the types of business entities allowed and a list of related filing fees.

## Sole Proprietorship

A sole proprietorship is a business that is owned by one person (or husband and wife). Although this is the easiest form of business to start, the income and losses are treated as yours personally and will be filed on a Schedule C along with your regular Form 1040 tax return. If your profits are minimal, you will actually be paying less in income taxes with this form of business than with a corporation. The advantage is that this is the easiest form of business to start. The biggest disadvantages include the fact that you are personally liable for any debts incurred or as a result of a legal claim against your business and the fact that a sole proprietorship offers no tax shelters. All profits are taxed as personal income.

## "S" Corporation?

S corporations qualify for all of the other advantages of a regular corporation; however, they are taxed as a partnership. The profits and losses of the corporation are "passed-through" directly to the shareholders' personal tax returns in an amount equal to their proportionate share of stock holdings with the corporation. This is advantageous if the shareholder does not qualify to be taxed in the highest bracket (35 percent if over $311,950 in income). If it does become desirable to terminate status as an "S" corporation, a revocation form must then be filed with the IRS.

## "C" Corporation

"C" corporation is a legal entity that is recognized by all states as a separate being from those who run it. It can enter into contracts, pay taxes, and is liable for debts and claims. A corporation's officers and directors are generally shielded from personal liability for the corporation's debts and losses, however, there are certain situations where this is not the case. Additionally, a shareholder's creditors cannot reach the assets of the corporation to satisfy its debts. All corporations are "C" corporations and will be taxed as such unless you specifically request another form of incorporation, such as an "S" corporation or a "LLC," which are treated differently for tax purposes.

## Limited Liability Company ("LLC")

A Limited Liability Company, or LLC, is a business structure best described as a hybrid between a partnership and a corporation that gives its owners the best of both worlds – a "pass through" of all profits and losses to the owners without taxation of the entity itself, as in a partnership, and a shield from personal liability, as in a corporation. An "S" corporation and a limited partnership also offer these advantages, but unlike an "S" corporation, a limited liability company is actually a non-corporate entity. State laws, which would require a board of directors, officers, and by-laws, do not apply.

Also, the owners of an LLC do not lose their limited liability status if they participate in the management of the corporation, unlike a limited partner. Further, unlike the stringent requirements of an "S" corporation, an LLC can have more than 35 shareholders, can have foreign owners, can have owners who are corporations or partnerships, and issue more than one class of stock.

If you are in doubt as to what type of business entity you need to form, check with a small business accountant or attorney. Make sure you explain your current financial situation and reveal any additional sources of income. You want every tax advantage possible and to ensure your personal assets are protected.

# Chapter 6

# *Training*

Probably the number one question that people ask me is, "Where did you go to culinary school?" My response is, "I didn't." Neither did any of the executives of the three primary personal chef associations. The great thing about the personal chef industry is that you do not need to hold a degree or be a certified chef to be successful. And, while I personally envy anyone that has received professional training through a credible culinary school or certification program, holding credentials does not guarantee success in the field nor will it matter to the majority of your customers.

I learned to cook from my grandparents and parents. I was always helping out in the kitchen. As a child, I would watch "The Galloping Gourmet" with Graham Kerr, "The Frugal Gourmet" with Jeff Smith, and, of course, Julia Child. My passion for cooking got a boost when cable television started airing cooking shows. I make time to watch the Food TV network. Besides the recipe ideas, I focus on technique, presentation, flavor combinations and more. It's really no different than taking a correspondence course. I learn better by watching a demonstration than by just reading.

# 20 Percent Cooking and 80 Percent Business

The experienced personal chef will tell you that, while cooking ability is obviously important, your success hinges on 80 percent business skills and 20 percent cooking skills. You could be the best cook in the world but unless you know how to market, sell, and tend to the details of your business, you will probably not succeed. However, you can be an average cook with self-taught cooking skills and make a decent living if you possess solid business and marketing skills.

With that said, I would encourage anyone who is considering entering into the profession to take classes or attend training that will round out their ability to successfully operate their business. Provided that you already know how to cook, this chapter focuses on some areas of study that need your attention if you want to operate a successful personal chef business.

## Marketing

Marketing is the one business skill subset that is most vital to your success. Marketing is everything you do to get people to purchase your product or service. Without marketing skills and a well-though-out marketing plan, you will struggle to get information about your business into the hands of prospective customers.

Marketing encompasses several elements, most of which involve communicating your message to prospective clients. It includes your business name, visual identity, brochures, press releases, business cards, print advertisements, radio & television commercials, direct mail, vehicle signs and more. Not only do you need to know something about each of these marketing elements, you also need to know how to implement them without spending thousands of dollars. You may only need to implement one or two of these strategies to launch your business. Or, you may go all out with a marketing blitz and then scale back your marketing efforts once you establish a solid client base.

Your local Chamber of Commerce, the Internet, library, business networking groups and personal chef associations are excellent resources that can provide information on developing and executing successful marketing programs. *Appendix C* is a worksheet that will help you better formulate your marketing strategy.

## Your New Sales Career

Selling is another vital skill that you must master before you can be successful. Getting a prospect to commit to try your service takes special skills. Any successful salesperson will tell you that listening to your prospects takes priority over telling them how wonderful you and your recipes are. A good sales person asks open-ended questions and then shuts up and listens while the client talks. By listening and understanding why the client believes she needs your service, you can focus on how your service can address those needs. If you can do that, you will get a new client almost every time – guaranteed!

I have been directly involved in sales for most of my career. I can honestly say that signing a new personal chef customer is the easiest sale I've ever closed. As a personal chef, I have closed more than 90 percent of my sales when I have been able to schedule a face-to-face appointment in the prospect's home. When trying to sell over the telephone, that percentage is probably more like 20 percent, still a respectable statistic in the sales world.

There are a variety of ways to learn sales skills. You can attend classes on selling that are offered by professional sales training companies – these are usually very expensive but worth it if you have the time and money. I prefer books or audiotapes. Some of my favorite authors of books on selling include Tom Hopkins, Harvey Mackay, and Joe Girard.

## Sound Business Practices

I know I've said this before, but I'll keep repeating it...being a great cook is not enough. You need to learn how to run a business. This includes funding, accounting, purchasing, customer service, budgeting, and all the other daily mundane tasks needed to make your business thrive. If you just like to cook and think you can get by without organizing your business, you won't be in business very long. Your local Chamber of Commerce or Small Business Administration can provide you with information and training on how to operate your business. There are also a variety of books and Internet resources available and they are listed in *Appendix D*.

## Food Safety

Food safety is a must. You need to learn how to properly prepare and handle food items to avoid contamination and food borne illnesses. Your local college, university or Board of Health will usually offer classes and food safety certifications. A list of resources is included in *Appendix B*.

## A Word About Training and Seminars

My advice, before investing a lot of money in seminars and training, especially for new personal chefs, make sure that you know what the tuition and fees include.  It may include membership in an association. This is fine if you intend to join that particular association.

There are other seminars and training programs available or soon to be available. These seminars and workshops are focused on topics such as career guidance, marketing, advertising, customer service, and sales. These affordable seminars are not affiliated with any of the associations or culinary schools. They are available to all personal chefs. For more information, visit www.personalchefmarketing.com.

## Chapter 7

# *Joining A Professional Association*

As with any industry or profession, there are a variety of resources that offer education and support to personal chefs. I made mention of the personal chef associations earlier and the role they have played in the history and development of the personal chef industry.

Keep in mind, however, that the personal chef industry is unregulated and membership in these associations is totally optional. Among the estimated 6,000 or so personal chefs operating businesses around the country today, I estimated that 4,500 belong to at least one of the associations. There are even a few who are members of multiple associations.

These associations can be beneficial if you are seeking educational opportunities or are in need of a support system to share ideas, find recipes, and tap into a variety of industry-specific resources.

## Support for U.S. Personal Chefs

Currently, there are three associations that offer membership services to personal chefs in the United States. The United States Personal Chef Association, American Personal Chef Association and the Personal Chefs Network.

While I am a strong proponent of joining a support organization, you need to join the one that is right for you. Choosing an association is one of the most important choices you can make. So, you need to research each one very carefully.

The first, and most important, fact to know about these associations is that each one currently operates as a for-profit business. They are owned and operated by people who are making their living by providing support to personal chefs. This is perfectly fine by me. These people are extremely passionate about the industry and are ready and willing to offer guidance and support to all personal chefs.

Other industries such as accounting, engineering, marketing, or manufacturing have not-for-profit associations that are directly or indirectly controlled by their members. In many instances, the members of not-for-profit professional associations elect or hire executives to oversee the day-to-day operations. These types of associations are responsible for developing, implementing and monitoring industry-wide certification standards. This is not the case in the personal chef industry.

There are no "industry standards" or one regulatory body overseeing the personal chef industry. Each personal chef association is individually owned and operated by entrepreneurs competing for your business.

## "Member" or "Customer?"

When you join one of these associations, are you a customer or a member? A customer is defined as "someone who pays for goods and services." It's no different than car dealerships, insurance companies or fast food restaurants competing for your hard earned dollar. Each one is going to try to sell you on their features and benefits. A member is someone who "belongs to a group or an association." Using these definitions, I think that you are a customer first, and a member, second. Your association should treat you as a customer because there are other associations competing for your business.

When researching associations, you need to separate the facts from the fluff. Having been employed in the marketing and advertising industry for most of my professional career, I know fluff when I see it. I've even created it. They'll give you dozens of reasons to join but won't tell you what their shortcomings are.

Like my grandpa use to say, "There are a thousand ways to skin a cat." I don't think he actually sat around skinning cats (at least I hope not). I think he meant everyone has their own ideas and methods of doing things. In the end, however, they all accomplish the same goal.

## Ask Around

If you want the inside scoop, interview a handful of personal chefs from each association. Ask for their honest opinion about what they like and don't like.

You'll discover that most personal chefs will speak candidly about their association. You will also find that many personal chefs have left one association to join another because they were simply looking for something different such as training, benefits, support services, networking and fellowship.

## Do What's Best for You

Do your homework and then join the association that best meets your criteria. Before becoming a personal chef, I conducted my own research and developed my own criteria for choosing to purchase a membership in a personal chef association.

Because I want to encourage you to make up your own mind about which of these associations to join, if any at all, I don't want to "officially" endorse any one specific association.

I joined the USPCA. My good friend Doug Gifford, who introduced me to the industry, is a member of the APCA while another friend, Greg Ryan, joined the PCN. We all enjoy many of the amenities and benefits of our memberships and are satisfied with how our associations are managed. I believe that each one has something to offer, generally works hard for its members and is moving the industry in the right direction.

As these associations compete for your business, you may encounter people with very strong beliefs served with a side dish of hostility toward another association. Friendly competition is good. Don't get caught up in the childish rhetoric. Tend to your own business.

> *The way to gain a good reputation is to endeavor to be what you desire to appear.*
>
> — *Socrates*

## Meet the Associations (in order of existence)

### United States Personal Chef Association

The United States Personal Chef Association was founded by David and Susan MacKay in 1991. They are credited with developing the personal chef business model and organizing the personal chef industry on a national level. Since 1991, the USPCA has enrolled approximately 5,500 members and reports that 2,376 personal chefs are active, dues paying members. Of those active members, approximately 60 percent are listed on the USPCA's personal chef locator web site, hireachef.com.

Membership dues are $299 per year. Initial membership fees are assessed for personal chefs who have not completed training through the USPCI (or Culinary Business Academy). A new personal chef without prior training can expect to pay for the Professional Personal Chef Reference Manual for $895. A personal chef with prior experience and training can join for $599 but must meet certain work-related requirements and complete the online testing. This allows personal chefs who have received training through another association or training program to join at a reduced rate.

The USPCA operates out of its own facility in Rio Rancho, New Mexico. Its staff consists of 12 full-time employees, three full time trainers and eight part-time employees.

In December 1996, the USPCA launched the United States Personal Chef Institute (now the Culinary Business Academy), its training entity. More than 720 personal chefs have completed the USPCI training program and earned their Certified Personal Chef (CPC) certification. The USPCA is the only association to have its own certification program. This program is trademarked and currently under review by the National Skills and Standards Board to be considered as a training standard for the personal chef industry. Currently, approximately 400 personal chefs are enrolled in the CPC certification program.

## American Personal Chef Association

The American Personal Chef Association was founded by personal chef Candy Wallace in 1995 after operating local and regional personal chef associations in San Diego, California. She then developed the American Personal Chef Institute a year later. The APCA does not audit its membership but reports that 3,215 people participate in the APCA online forums on the association's web site. The initial fee to join the APCA is $275 (requires documented proof of operating a personal chef business a minimum of 6 months) with an annual renewal fee of $150. Membership is included with purchase of APCA training programs starting at $650. The APCA employs a support staff of five. While it does not have its own culinary training program, it contracts four trainers/regional managers. It also offers a "Train-the-Trainer" program for culinary school instructors who offer the APCA personal chef operations training program.

The APCA offers a two-day seminar for new or aspiring personal chefs. The cost of this seminar is currently $995 and includes membership in the APCA.

APCA members receive a discount when they pursue either of the two American Culinary Federation's personal chef certifications that were developed with input from the APCA and were implemented in January of 2003.

### Personal Chefs Network

Sharon Worster and Wendy Perry formed the Personal Chefs Network, Inc. in February 2000. The PCN has an active membership of over 600. Approximately 50 percent of those members are listed on their personal chef locator, accessible through their web site at personalchefsnetwork.com. Annual dues are currently $145.00, with a fee of $650.00 required to join initially. PCN does not offer a certification program but offers its own training course, online workshops and a press release service, all included with membership. It prides itself on providing personal support to new and experienced personal chefs.

Comparatively Speaking

Here is a benefits comparison chart that I put together based on information promotional materials and input from each association. Some benefits may require additional investment.

| Benefit | APCA | PCN | USPCA |
|---|---|---|---|
| JoiningFees(Membership & Training) | $695 | $650 | $895 |
| Annual Dues | $150 | $145 | $299 |
| Training Course | ♦ | ♦ | ♦ |
| Group Liability Insurance | | | ♦ |
| Proprietary Certification | | | ♦ |
| Third Party Certification * | ♦ | ♦ | ♦ |
| Online Testing | | | ♦ |
| Hands-On Culinary Classes | | | ♦ |
| Business Training Classes | ♦ | ♦ | ♦ |
| Workshops/Conventions | ♦ | ♦ | ♦ |
| Online Seminars | | ♦ | |
| Magazine/Newsletter | ♦ | ♦ | ♦ |
| Marketing Support | ♦ | ♦ | ♦ |
| Lead Referral | ♦ | ♦ | ♦ |
| Free Member Web site | ♦ | ♦ | ♦ |
| Online Member Forums | ♦ | ♦ | ♦ |
| Local/Regional Chapters | ♦ | ♦ | ♦ |
| Recipe Exchange | ♦ | ♦ | ♦ |
| Recipe Software | ♦ | ♦ | ♦ |
| Advisory Council | ♦ | ♦ | ♦ |

* Third party certification is available to all personal chefs through the American Culinary Federation. Fees discounted to APCA members through special partnership agreement.

38

# Chapter 8

# *Opinions On Certification*

So, how important is professional training and certification in the personal chef industry? It depends whom you ask.

## Where the Leaders Stand

Ask the owners of any of the personal chef associations and they would be justified to cast a vote in favor of certification. This is why Candy Wallace, executive director of the American Personal Chef Association spent six years trying to convince the American Culinary Federation that the personal chef is a legitimate culinary profession. It's also the reason David MacKay of the United States Personal Chef Association has been working diligently to get the National Skills and Standards Board to adopt the USPCA training program as a federally recognized industry standard for certifying personal chefs. Sharon Worster and Wendy Perry of the Personal Chefs Network do not emphasize certification but do value the importance of training. Each association has its own training materials for which they've invested a lot of time and money developing. They sell these training and support materials to members. This is one of the primary ways they make money.

## Your Peers Are Split

I've encountered personal chefs who will argue that you have to be certified to be successful. Others will tell you that it just doesn't matter. Many personal chefs have invested a lot of money and time in training and certification. They won't hold back their opinion that anybody who doesn't plunk down thousands of dollars for training manuals, classes and certification isn't worthy of being called a personal chef. While I disagree with them, I respect their educational accomplishments and commitment to their craft. However, I can still call myself a personal chef and so can you. Although I haven't purchased the training materials or taken certification exams, I completed my college education; not to mention hundreds of hours researching recipes, watching cooking programs on television, testing recipes in my own kitchen, educating myself on food safety and filling in any of the blanks that may have existed prior to launching a successful business.

## Only My Opinion

I take nothing away from any personal chef who is certified or holds a culinary degree. I commend them for their hard work and dedication to their profession. But, I will honestly say that my clients do not care whether I am certified or not. It has never become an issue. They only care that I possess the skills to cook healthy, delicious meals that are properly prepared and packaged. They are more concerned that I run a clean, ethical business and can accommodate their requests. I am extremely confident in my abilities to cook as well as market and operate a successful, trustworthy business.

I don't believe that adding letters or initials after my name will make me a better personal chef or result in me making more money. My wife is a Certified Public Accountant. She worked hard to earn her CPA designation; which is extremely important to her career and gives her credibility amongst her peers. To pursue any type of certification at this point in my career, however, would be purely for personal satisfaction.

# The Future

I believe that for the industry to evolve, the personal chef industry needs to have the foresight that the American Culinary Federation had when it was formed. Three separate, competing organizations came together for the good of the industry to form an alliance to advance the plight of professional chefs and cooks on all levels. I'm sure this wasn't easy and required a lot of negotiation and discussion about the purpose and goals of such an alliance.

The personal chef associations continue to compete at varying degrees of intensity. In my opinion, the industry has a strong foothold and it's time to move forward. I believe that friendly competition is good and encourages the constant development of new ideas. But, a fragmented industry will only stagnate growth. It would just take one or two individuals to step forward and organize a joint effort to keep the momentum moving in a positive direction.

# Chapter 9

# *Certification Options*

If you decide to become certified, you need to know what options you have. There are personal chef training programs being added to curriculums at colleges, universities and trade schools all over the country. Many of these programs have their own certification designations or give you the tools you need to pursue certification through one of the personal chef associations or their partners. There are two primary certification programs that I believe are going to be the benchmarks for the personal chef industry. Those are the USPCA program and the new ACF programs.

## American Culinary Federation Certification

The American Culinary Federation (ACF), Inc., a professional, not-for-profit association for chefs and cooks, was founded in 1929 in New York City by three chefs' associations: the Société Culinaire Philanthropique, the Vatel Club, and the Chefs Association of America. The principal goal of the founding chefs remains true to ACF today—to promote the professional image of American chefs worldwide through education among culinarians at all levels, from apprentices to the most accomplished certified master chefs.

ACF is the largest and most prestigious association dedicated to professional chefs in the United States today. It was the pioneer responsible for elevating the position of executive chef from service status to the professional category in the U.S. Department of Labor's *Dictionary of Official Titles* in 1976.

In August of 2002 the ACF announced a partnership with the APCA and the addition of two certification levels for personal chefs. The ACF requirements to attain these levels of certification are as follows:

### Personal Certified Executive Chef (PCEC)

A chef with advanced culinary skills and a minimum of seven (7) years of professional cooking experience with a minimum of two years as a personal chef; provides cooking services on a "cook-for-hire-basis" to a variety of clients; responsible for menu planning and development, marketing, financial management and operational decisions; provides nutritious, safe, eye-appealing, and properly flavored foods.

### Personal Certified Chef  (PCC)

A chef with a minimum of four (4) years of professional cooking experience with a minimum of one (1) full year employed as a personal chef who is engaged in the preparation, cooking, serving, and sorting of foods on a "cook-for-hire basis"; responsible for menu planning and development, marketing, financial management and operational decisions of private business; provides cooking services to a variety of clients; possesses a thorough knowledge of food safety and sanitation and culinary nutrition.

#### About the ACF Certification

The American Culinary Federation certification program for personal chefs is open to all personal chefs. According to Marilyn Burchfield who oversees the ACF certification programs, no applications have been received for ACF certification as of December of 2003.

Burchfield acknowledges that, besides cost and the fact that certification is not an industry requirement, there may be a misconception about the time it takes to become certified. ACF certification is not necessarily a 3–6 year process.

If a personal chef meets the minimum requirements, including education, training and job experience, the candidate can apply for certification. They must then successfully complete the required written and practical exams. Therefore, a personal chef can become certified in just a few months. It's the education and training that may require a significant time investment.

## USPCA Certification

### *Certified Personal Chef (CPC)*

In 1996 the United States Personal Chef Association, as the industry leader, created their Certified Personal Chef (CPC) program with a three-fold purpose:

- To provide a standard by which the public could assess a personal chef's competency.

- To provide the personal chef with industry recognition of their professional commitment.

- To establish standards by which the personal chef industry could become self-regulated.

The Certified Personal Chef (CPC) designation is an industry endorsement of professional expertise. Certified Personal Chef (CPC) clients are assured of a commitment to excellent service. It is an extra point of differentiation and tangible evidence of knowledge that will help market your services.

The Certified Personal Chef designation is a performance-based certification. Although formal and culinary education play a part in the success of a personal chef, how the personal chef performs his or her duties is more heavily weighted in the personal chef certification evaluation process.

The Certification Program requirements, standards and procedures are established by the USPCA's National Advisory council and may be changed without notice to reflect, support and enhance the industry's growth.

# Chapter 10

# *Your Time Commitment*

People become personal chefs for various reasons. Some just love to cook and want to make money at their craft. Some are culinary professionals tired of the long days and late hours of cooking in a restaurant. While others, like me, are burnt out on corporate America and are seeking a career change doing something they enjoy and are good at. The great thing about being a personal chef is that you can ease into it slowly over a few months to a year, or you can take the plunge and dedicate yourself to working full time.

## Easing Into It Part Time

If you are currently employed and have a source of income, you may want to build your business slowly so that you aren't overwhelmed, mentally and financially. There are a lot of variables such as location, the economy, competition and your marketing abilities that will have either a negative or positive impact on your short-term business growth. If you work a full-time, 40-hour workweek, you may be limited to cooking in the evening hours or on weekends. However, it might be hard to find clients who are willing to work out this type of cooking arrangement.

If you work part-time, you can easily split your day or week to accommodate a cooking schedule that will be acceptable to your clients. My cook day usually starts around 7:00 a.m., when I do my grocery shopping, and generally ends around 2:00 p.m. This type of schedule would allow you to work a part-time evening or weekend job. Or, if you work two or three full, 8-hour days at your part-time job, you can schedule cook days on your days off.

## Full Time, Full Speed Ahead

When I started my personal chef business, I had been downsized and was suddenly faced with the need to replace a decent income. It was sink or swim. So, using my marketing skills, I was able to launch my business in a few short weeks. However, I had done a considerable amount of research about the personal chef industry because I knew that I was facing possible unemployment. I already made up my mind to become a personal chef. As fate would have it, I just had to do it sooner and quicker than expected.

If you are going to go into this full time, do so with a plan in place. You need to have cash reserves or a source of income to cover your bills for at least three months. You don't want to lose your house, car or, even worse, your family. You also need a business plan and, especially, a marketing plan.  If you don't have your personal chef business up and running with a good income stream within three months (six months, tops!) you may need to develop your business part time or find another line of work.

# Chapter 11

# *Establishing Your Identity*

## Naming Your Business

Go to any of the professional chef association web sites or to your telephone book and look up the names of personal chef businesses. Some are predictable and boring. While others are so cutesy that you don't even recognize them as a personal chef business. Others, however, are very creative and well thought out.

What makes a good business name? I have been involved in naming or renaming several businesses and products. Naming a business is as important as naming a child. I believe that you should check your ego at the door when naming your personal chef business. If your name is Bob, "Bob's Personal Chef Service" is not too creative; but I guess it works. If you are lucky, you may have a name (or at least a nickname) that can be related to food or cooking. For example, "Rosemary" is a no-brainer as is "Cookie" or "Barbie" (think Barbi-Q). A good friend of mine, Douglas Gifford, uses his middle name Caesar. His business is called Chef Caesar's Cuisine, a very culinary-friendly business name.

Names can also be too long. "I Want to Cook Your Supper" is a long name. If you were selling tires, you could maybe get away with having a longer business name like "Bob's High Quality Refurbished Tires." But, because the personal chef business takes some explaining, you have already used up three words (personal chef service). "I Want to Cook Your Supper Personal Chef Service" is, in my opinion, too wordy and doesn't fit too well on a business card.

When I named my business, I wanted to not only create a name people could easily remember, I also wanted to create a persona. Inspired by "The Galloping Gourmet", "The Frugal Gourmet", "Mr. Food", "The Surreal Chef", and "The Naked Chef," I decided on "Doctor Dinner" and my tag line would be, "A real lifesaver in the kitchen!"

"Doctor Dinner" is fun for me because people call me by that name. When I shop at the store, the employees refer to me as "Doc" or "Doctor Dinner". It also comes in handy when I make television appearances, do cooking demonstrations and write magazine articles. I have clients that still refer to me as "Doctor Dinner" and can't remember my first name.

## Check Name Availability

Another chef in Atlanta, Mike McCurdy named his business "The Dinner Doctor". Fortunately, he lives far enough away that we do not compete for business. This is why it is important to register your business name in your state. If "The Dinner Doctor" operated his business in Indiana, there would be a lot of confusion and it could have led to a battle for the name in court..

## Tired and Overused Names

You should also avoid using overused cooking-related terms. Probably the most overused word when naming a personal business is "Thyme". "Dinner Thyme", "Supper Thyme", "Meal Thyme", "Just In Thyme", "Thyme for Yourself"... Get the point?

If you are going to name your business, make a list of names. Test out the name on friends, family and even strangers. If there is any question as to what the name means or appears to confuse people, don't use it! Move on down the list until you find something that feels comfortable. You'll know it when you hear it. It will just feel right.

# Chapter 12

# *Tools of the Trade*

As a personal chef, you will experience a lot of different situations and cooking environments. I've cooked in a small apartment galley kitchen where I was barely able to turn around. I've also cooked in kitchens that were so large, I felt like I had run a marathon by the end of the day. Each kitchen is different as are the types of cook tops, ovens, cutlery and cookware people have in their kitchens. That's why it is so important to make sure you at least use tools that are familiar to you. Knowing how your cookware reacts to cooking with gas or electricity will help you maintain some consistency when cooking. And, there is nothing more frustrating than trying to slice tomatoes or potatoes with a client's dull chef's knife. You need quality cookware and tools to take to each job.

## Cookware

First, you need to make sure you purchase or have access to a good set of cookware that will see a lot of use, but will also stand up under the stress of being banged around during transport.

My first set of cookware that I used was a Christmas present from my parents. They had no idea that I was considering becoming a personal chef. It's a set of very durable *Wolfgang Puck®* cookware. It has glass lids that are very heavy. I packed that set of cookware in a plastic tub that I carried into my clients' homes. This put a lot of strain on my back and caused a lot of sleepless nights.

I use a set of commercial grade 18/10 stainless steel All-Clad cookware with metal lids. I highly recommend All-Clad. If you watch cooking shows on television or visit almost any commercial kitchen, you will most likely find All-Clad cookware being used. Not only is it high quality, but it also carries a lifetime warranty. Visit them at www.allclad.com.

I now pack my cookware in a large duffle bag that has wheels. Being able to wheel my cookware into the client's home has eliminated the strain on my back. A good set of commercial grade cookware can range from $500 to $1,500. At minimum, you need a small frying pan, a large skillet, a couple of saucepans and a stockpot or Dutch oven. I also have a wok for the stir-fry and Asian dishes I prepare.

Visit www.personalchefmarketing.com for a list of resources offering excellent pricing on a variety of quality cookware including All-Clad.

## Cutlery

Almost as important as your cookware is your cutlery. I learned early on that you can't, and shouldn't, rely on your clients to have a good set of knives on hand.

I carry just three knives with me when I cook; a paring knife, a boning knife and an 8-inch chef's knife. I also carry a sharpener and sharpen them prior to each use. A dull knife can make for a long day because it not only takes you longer to cut meats and vegetables, but you can also actually damage what you are cutting if the blade is dull. Knives can be rather expensive, costing you between $25 and $300 each. You don't have to get the best knives when first starting out. Save up and reward yourself once your business is booming.

I use professional chef knives from the F. Dick Company. They have been manufacturing the highest quality knives and tools for chefs and butchers in Germany since 1778. More professional chefs use F. Dick cutlery than any other brand. For more information on the F. Dick line of cutlery, visit www. personalchefmarketing.com.

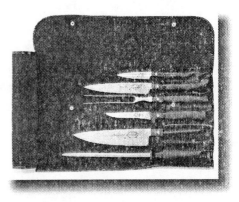

You also need a good cutting board that meets food safety standards. There has been much discussion about the use of wooden cutting boards and their health risks. There are cutting boards made out of non-porous, lightweight plastic materials that can be easily cleaned. Look for cutting boards approved for commercial food preparation use. You can purchase a cutting board for about $25.

## Basic Utensils

I also carry a few utensils with me just in case my client doesn't have what I need. I include a spatula, slotted spoon, stirring spoons, tongs and a potato masher. My favorite store to purchase utensils is the dollar store, where each one costs, well...a dollar!

## Other Gadgets and Gizmos

As far as kitchen gadgets, I have a propensity to get caught up watching those late night info-mercials where they peddle vegetable choppers, spaghetti strainers, and other "space age" gadgets that supposedly make life easier. It wasn't long before I was toting a box full of goofy gadgets that actually took me longer to assemble, wash and disassemble than if I had just used the basic tools like a knife, tongs or colander. The only gadget I carry with me is a small electric hand blender, or what Chef Emeril Lagasse refers to as a "boat motor."

## Spices & Oils

You need to take your own spices and oils to your client's house. Chances are, the spices, oils and other ingredients your client has on hand are old. If spices are old, they lose their aroma and flavor. I always carry the following spices, herbs, extracts, oils, vinegars and wines with me:

### Spices & Extracts

Allspice
Arrowroot
Basil
Bay Leaves
Black Pepper
Caraway Seed
Cayenne Pepper
Celery Seed
Chinese Five Spice
Chile Powder
Chives
Cilantro
Cinnamon
Coriander
Coriander Seed
Cream of Tartar
Cumin
Curry.
Dill
Dill Seed

Fennel
Garlic
Ginger
Italian Seasoning
Lemon Pepper
Marjoram
Mint
Mustard Seeds
Mustard Powder
Nutmeg
Onion
Oregano
Paprika
Parsley
Poppy Seed
Poultry Seasoning
Red Pepper
Rosemary
Sage
Salt

Seasoned Salt
Sesame Seed
Tarragon
Thyme

### Oils, Vinegars & Wines

Olive Oil
Canola Oil
Sesame Oil
Pepper Oil
Red Wine Vinegar
White Wine Vinegar
Balsamic Vinegar
Cooking Sherry
White Wine
Red Wine

# Transporting Your Tools and Ingredients

Being a personal chef requires a lot of lifting. If you aren't careful, you could easily injure your back. When I first started my business, I purchased small plastic tubs and crammed everything I could into them. I had one tub each for spices, oils, dry goods, utensils, and cookware. I was making several trips back and forth from the client's house to the van carrying these tubs which weighed 25 to 30 pounds each. It didn't take too many nights sleeping on a heating pad and going through a jar of analgesic ointment to figure out that there had to be a better way.

Now, I put my cookware, towels and cleaning supplies in a large duffle bag that has wheels. I can drag it out of my van and pull it all of the way to the client's kitchen. The only time I lift it is to put it back into the van.

As far as my spices, oils, utensils and other ingredients, I have discovered the greatest product for personal chefs. It is so wonderful, in fact, that I contacted the manufacturer and have the rights to market this product. The **Port-O-Pantry**™ is a durable, light-weight plastic tool chest on wheels that has enough storage space for your spices, oils, cutlery, utensils and more. You can ease it, fully loaded, out of your vehicle and roll it right into the client's kitchen. I set mine in the kitchen and can quickly access everything I need. It weighs about 50 pounds when fully loaded.

*The Port-O-Pantry™ helps personal chefs organize spices, oils, utensils, cutlery and small appliances. It's lightweight and extremely easy to roll right into the client's home.*

For more information on the *Port-O-Pantry™*, visit www.personalchefmarketing.com

# Chapter 13

# *Playing It Safe*

I can't say enough about the need to follow proper food handling and preparation guidelines to prevent food borne illness. Your local board of health can provide you with information on food safety courses in your area.

## ServSafe®

ServSafe® is a food safety certification course developed by the National Restaurant Association Educational Foundation (NRAEF) that is offered nationwide and administered several times a year in most cities. This course is usually offered over a couple of days with a test administered upon completion. A passing grade results in receiving certification.

The last thing you want to have happen is for your clients getting sick as a result of your carelessness or lack of knowledge when it comes to food safety.

If for some reason, you cannot take this course immediately, there are various books, publications and web sites that provide important guidelines for handling and preparing food. Appendix

B lists a number of Internet web sites that provide valuable food safety information and links to other resources.

# Chapter 14
# Covering Your Assets

## Insuring Your Business

As with any business, you need to be insured against any possible negligence on your part. Even though you may choose to form a business entity that limits your personal liability, such as a corporation or LLC, you don't want to risk losing any assets your business has, not to mention tarnishing your reputation. Therefore, it is critical that you find an insurer who is willing to underwrite a personal chef policy.

That, however, is easier said than done. I could not find a local insurance company in Indianapolis to insure my business, at least at a reasonable price. The APCA and PCN can recommend insurers.

The USPCA currently includes basic liability insurance coverage as part of its membership. This policy has many restriction and should be supplemented with a full-featured business owner's policy.

If you do find a policy, it may be limited in scope to only cover you while you are cooking in a client's home. These policies usually just cover damage to a client's property. For example, if you damage a counter top or catch the kitchen on fire, you may be covered up to a certain amount. Accidents do happen and its wise to have some type of coverage.

While membership fees in a personal chef associations may include insurance coverage, you should expect to pay anywhere between $400 and $1,500 per year for small business liability insurance, depending on the amount of coverage, type of coverage and your deductible.

For information about insurance for your personal chef business, visit www.personalchefmarketing.com.

# Chapter 15

# *Finding Recipes*

Before you set out to find clients, you need to know what you are going to offer in the way of a menu. Are you going to offer standard fare and comfort foods? Or, are you going to offer special menus for diabetics, vegetarians and other people with special dietary needs?

Whatever your goal, you need to assemble a menu that offers a variety of tasty, nutritious and freezer-friendly choices. You need to include chicken, beef, pork, fish, vegetables, soups, salads, sandwiches and breads.

## Association Recipes

One of the advantages of joining one of the personal chef associations is that they can provide you with kitchen-tested recipes specifically designed for personal chefs. These recipes are usually provided in printed form and on CD-ROM and may include software programs that allow you to manipulate the recipes, generate shopping lists, manage your pantry inventory and more. A drawback is that you may be required to pay extra for the recipes and software; another investment that can add to startup costs.

## Your Own Recipes

Before putting my menu together, I researched the types of food items and ingredients that can and can't be frozen. I then found recipes using a variety of resources including books, magazines and web sites that offered freezer-friendly recipes. While it was labor intensive, I didn't have to shell out hundreds of dollars. I also downloaded free shareware computer programs that allow me to manage my recipes, menu and shopping lists. It pays to be resourceful and patient.

My menu contains nearly 250 menu items, only of which about 75 are chosen on a regular basis. Most of my clients tend to choose items that are fairly common and will order these items time and time again, occasionally trying something new. Sometimes, I will even include an item, at no extra charge, that I think they might like. I found many of my recipes on www.cooksrecipes.com, an excellent web site with more than 12,000 recipes, cooking tips, culinary dictionary and charts. I include some of my clients' favorite recipes in *Appendix F*.

## Chapter 16

# *Developing Your Services*

As a personal chef, you need to determine what types of products and services you are going to offer. You can stick with the basic personal chef services or you can branch out and offer a variety of "add-on" services and products.

## In-Home Personal Chef Service

Most personal chefs offer the standard in-home meal preparation service. You go into you client's home and prepare a number of packaged meals that can be reheated and served at a later time. This may include a weekly service, bi-weekly service, monthly service or on an as-needed basis. I have a few clients that I only cook for when their life gets hectic.

## Meal Delivery

Some personal chefs have access to commercial kitchens. These kitchens are either their own or leased from a local restaurant, church, clubhouse or other facility. These kitchens must be approved for commercial use by local health departments and are usually subject to inspection without any advance notice.

Check with local health departments and review all applicable health codes prior to jumping into this type of arrangement.

In this case, you would offer a more limited menu to your clients and they would place an order for meals. You would prepare these meals and deliver them to your clients home and either refrigerate or freeze them. You might offer this type of service once a week, once every two weeks or you might even prepare daily meals and deliver them fresh in the afternoon or close to dinner time.

## Weekly Service

Some clients may want you to prepare meals once a week. A client will usually request this service because they do not want the meals to be frozen. They desire fresh meals that don't have to be thawed before reheating. Many personal chefs consider this to be a premium service and price it as such. You would be preparing one entrée for each night as well as one or two side dishes and possibly salads and breads. It really depends on what the client desires. This type of client requires a lot of attention. They may want to choose from a standard menu or have you customize their menu.

## Bi-Weekly Service

A bi-weekly service means that you prepare meals every two weeks. You can freeze all of the meals or put the first week's meals in the refrigerator and the second week's meals in the freezer. Some clients will select a bi-weekly service but only have you cook once every four weeks. They might prefer this type of arrangement if they either travel frequently or are able to prepare meals on their own a few nights each week.

It is standard to offer a 5x2 (five by two) service. You would prepare five entrees and five side dishes and double the servings. For example, if they choose lasagna, they would have lasagna for two nights. The same goes for the side dish. If they pick green beans with almonds, they would have two night's worth. I never package the sides with the entrees. This helps break up the monotony of having the same side and entrée. They can then mix and match their items. Some clients may not want to repeat. Let's say, for example, you charge $300 for a 5x2 service. You could add $100 for a 10x1 service and add an additional $79 per person. You really don't have any additional ingredient costs for a 10x1 over a 5x2. So, if there are four people in the family, and you prepare a 10x1 service, you would charge $558.

## Monthly Service

This is similar to the bi-weekly service but you are preparing a month's worth of meals (or twenty meals). Again, many personal chefs use the 5x4 (five by four) model. They prepare five entrees and five side items and multiply it by four. Using the same example as the 5x2 service, your client would have four nights worth of lasagna and four nights worth of green beans with almonds.

I charge additional for a 10x2 in which the client gets a choice of 10 different entrees and 10 different sides. Both are doubled, meaning they would repeat the meals every two weeks. I would not recommend trying to cook 20 different sides and entrees. You won't have enough time and you will go crazy trying to accomplish this amazing feat. However, if you think you can pull it off, charge extra for this service.

Some clients may desire this service monthly or once every two months if they have time to cook or they travel and can't eat at home.

## Guarantee

I guarantee my meals for 45 days. I do this for a couple of reasons. First, I believe this is reasonable. Things can get freezer burn or go bad if frozen too long. The other reason is that I want my clients to consume the meals quickly so that they need my service again. Under my guarantee, I will replace a meal if it has something wrong with it such as freezer burn or another anomaly. I tell them to put the item in the refrigerator and call me. I will come and pick it up and find out what went wrong so that it won't happen again. However, if they just don't like the meal because of how it tastes, then I will not replace it if I followed the recipe.

## Parties

Besides offering your standard services, you will also find that parties are an excellent source of income. You will get inquiries about dinner parties, birthday parties, anniversaries, intimate dinners, luncheons, breakfasts and more. If you do plan on doing these types of events, you need to determine what size of events you can handle by yourself and what types of events require you to hire additional help.

## Additional Products and Services

Some personal chefs offer additional services that relate to their business. Here are a few ideas.

### Bartending

If you have bartending experience or possess a decent knowledge about wine and spirits, you can tend bar at a party or event. You need to check with your State agency that issues licenses for this type of business activity. Fees for permits can run between $25 to $50 and are usually valid for one to three years. Make sure you know the regulations and absolutely know when to recognize someone who has had too much to drink. You could be liable if you serve alcohol to someone who ends up injuring themselves or someone else or causing a death. Make sure your insurance policy covers this type of work.

### Grocery Shopping Service

You can provide a grocery shopping service. Besides picking up food and ingredients for their cook day, add an additional cost to pick up any other items that they may need including snacks, wine, laundry detergent, toiletries, paper goods, and more. Charge them for the cost of those extra groceries plus a flat fee, perhaps $30 to $50. Some people may just want you to do their grocery shopping. I've seen people charge anywhere between $30 to $50 per hour plus the cost of groceries.

## Errand Service

How many times have you wished someone else could pick up your dry cleaning or a prescription or take that stack of videos back to the video store. You can come up with a list of errands. Be prepared for your clients to challenge you with errands you've never even thought about. Just make sure the errands are legal and you know what you are delivering or picking up!

## Demonstration Chef

Go to your local supermarket, appliance store or kitchen supply store and offer to do cooking demonstrations using their products. A hardware store or garden shop could benefit by having you cook burgers, hot dogs or other items on their new line of gas grills or smokers. Get creative.

## Cooking Instructor

Offer to present cooking classes at a local gourmet kitchen, school, community college or in your client's home. Check to see if local social service organization could use help teaching cooking skills to people with disabilities. Pricing can be an hourly rate plus supplies.

## Party Help

What's the point in throwing a party if you have to spend the whole time refilling the chip bowl, serving drinks or picking up empty plates and glasses? You may not be asked to cook, but your client may just want you there to serve and clean up. This is a great add-on business opportunity. Actually, cleaning up is the part of being a personal chef that I could really do without. A lady at the church I attend recently started a business called Party Hands. She doesn't cook but she helps serve and clean up after the party or event is over. You can bet that I will be using her service quite a bit to help me out when I need it.

### Kitchen Organizer

Help your clients by organizing their kitchen cabinets, refrigerator, freezer and pantry. Chances are, they've got items that have expired or forgot they had. This may be a full-day job. Make sure you charge an appropriate fee.

### Tailgate Cook

Local colleges, universities and professional sporting venues are places where people gather before an event to socialize, eat and drink. Attend these events to prospect. Look for the bigger parties, give them your business card and offer your services for future events. The group hosting the event may choose to pay you outright or everyone in their group can share the cost. If it's an event you would like to attend, offer to trade your services for a ticket or two to the game.

### Vacation Chef

Who wants to go on vacation and cook or spend every evening eating out at expensive restaurants? If you live in a tourist area, advertise your services to resorts, condos, or guest houses. If you have a client that is going on a vacation, tell them that you'll be happy to travel with them. Some personal chefs have found work cooking on sailboats and yachts or in cabins and summer homes. Some have even served as camp cooks on hiking and camping trips.

### Distributor

Another way to generate income is to sell products. The internet is a great source for companies looking for independent distributors of a variety of products ranging from vitamins, supplements and organic foods to cookware, cutlery, kitchen gadgets and appliances.

# Chapter 17

# *Pricing Your Services*

Pricing your services is one of the most difficult tasks you will face as a business owner. On one hand, you want to make a profit. On the other hand, you don't want to scare people away. You need to establish a price that will you to attract and maintain business.

## Hourly Rate Plus Groceries

There are a couple of different ways to price your services. Some personal chefs separate the cost of groceries from their service fee. They get reimbursed for the groceries and then charge either a flat rate or an hourly rate. For example, the groceries may cost $150 and the hourly fee is $30. For a 7-hour cookday from 8:00 a.m. to 3:00 p.m., the fee would be $210.

The problem with this model is that you must work more hours or set your hourly rate higher to meet your financial goal.

## Flat Rate Plus Groceries

Another way is to charge for groceries and then charge a flat fee of, say, $200. If the cook day is seven hours long, the hourly rate calculates to about $28 per hour. If the cook day is five hours, the hourly rate climbs to $40.

If you have a menu that requires more preparation and cook time, your hourly wage drops with each hour.

## Flat Fee – Groceries Included

Some personal chefs charge a flat rate for two people based on either a bi-weekly or monthly service and include the cost of groceries in the fee. They then charge a flat rate for each extra person. For example, if you charge $300 and only spend $100 on groceries, you net $200.

I prefer to use a hybrid of this method because I am pretty thrifty when it comes to shopping. I often get discounts on produce and meat because of the relationships I've established with the produce manager and meat managers at my favorite supermarket.

Because I try to primarily cook for families of four or more, I almost always meet or beat my target profit margin. Sometimes, that profit margin has been as high as $500 for one cook day; it was a monthly service for a large family that picked low-cost menu items. As I've gained more experience and have learned how to be more efficient in the kitchen, I've trimmed my cook day from about 10 hours down to about six hours.

## Sales Tax Issue

One of the factors that will make a difference when pricing your service is to understand what sales tax requirements, if any, your state places on your business. Each state's tax codes are different and subject to interpretation.

Some states require you to pay sales tax if you purchase the groceries for your client. The problem here is that, unless you are tax exempt, you get double-taxed; once when you purchase the groceries and again when you pay the tax on the money you receive from your client. Other states require you to just pay tax on the money you receive for groceries. Yet, other states view what you do as a service and don't require you to pay sales tax. When in doubt, hire an accountant or request a written explanation of your state's sales tax requirements.

## Pricing for Parties and Private Dinners

Setting a price for these types of events can be tricky and you can actually lose money if you aren't careful. One way to price these types of events is to charge a per person cost. To do this, you need to accurately estimate your food costs in advance as well as any other costs such as serving supplies, paper goods, additional help, etc. Once you calculate the total cost, you need to determine what you want your profit margin percentage to be. The problem with this method is that it takes a lot of work on your part to research the cost of ingredients and then adjust the numbers to make them come out right. If it's a large event, however, you will want to use this method.

You can cut into your profit margins if you don't calculate the markup correctly. Refer to the example below. Let's say you want a profit margin of 45 percent. The common mistake is to take the Cost Per Person (CPP) of $6.85 and multiply it by .45. This would be $3.08. If you add this amount to the CPP, you would charge $9.93 per person. However, your profit margin is actually only 31 percent. You are pricing your product at 45 percent of cost instead of a true 45 percent profit margin.

To figure out what you need your markup to be, divide the CPP by 100 minus DM and multiply that number by 100. In our example, that would be $6.85/(100-45)x100. The total price you would charge per person is $12.45. Your markup is $5.60 which is your desired profit margin of 45 percent.

Based on 100 guests, your total profit would be $308.00 if you use the wrong calculation. If you use the margin markup calculation, you would profit $560.00, a difference of $252!

| Items | Unit Price | *Net Cost |
|---|---|---|
| Chicken Breasts | $  0.75 | $   75.00 |
| Baby Carrots | $  0.25 | $   25.00 |
| Potatoes | $  0.25 | $   25.00 |
| Apple Pie | $  1.00 | $  100.00 |
| Iced Tea | $  0.25 | $   25.00 |
| Bottled Water | $  0.75 | $   75.00 |
| Coffee | $  0.10 | $   10.00 |
| Supplies | $ | $  150.00 |
| Staff | $ | $  200.00 |

| | | |
|---|---|---|
| Net Total | | $  685.00 |
| (CPP) Cost Per Person | | $    6.85 |
| (DM) Desired Margin | | 45% |
| (PPP) Price Per Person | | $   12.45 |
| Profit x 100 | | $  560.00 |

Price Per Person = CPP/(100-DM)x100
**based on 100 guests*

Another method, which I use for smaller events, is to charge an hourly rate plus the cost of groceries. I also charge an hourly rate for any extra help I may need to hire. I mark that cost up for a 20- to 30-percent profit margin. This method works great for smaller parties of 12 or less. I have a three-hour minimum. Here is how this method looks on paper. In this example, I charge $50/hour for four hours. Also, I hire a server at $15/hour and charge $25/ hour. This party cost the host about $35 per guest.

| Items | Unit Price | *Net Cost |
|---|---|---|
| My Labor Cost | $50 .00 | $  200.00 |
| Extra Labor | $25.00 | $  100.00 |
| Groceries | $125.00 | $  125.00 |

| | | |
|---|---|---|
| Net Total | | $  425.00 |
| Costs | | $  195.00 |
| Margin | | 54% |
| Profit | | $  230.00 |

**based on 12 guests**

# Chapter 18

# *Marketing Is the Key*

I am not going to launch into a full-blown marketing course. That's another book all by itself. You do need to know, however, that unless you know what marketing is and how it drives your business, you are headed for disaster. Each year, U.S. companies spend billions of dollars on marketing. You, need to know how to successfully market your business on a much smaller budget.

## Marketing Simply Defined

Marketing is the movement of products or services from the producer to the consumer. As a business function, marketing is a series of activities you implement to make your business visible to prospective clients. It includes planning, research, testing, creative development, advertising, analyzing and reworking your plan. It sounds difficult and complicated, but it doesn't have to be if you just understand the basic principles. You also need to understand that, as a personal chef, you do not need to spend a lot of money if you are willing to do some of the work yourself. You can even trade your service for the services of a graphic artist, writer, web site designer, or others that can help you implement elements of your marketing plan.

## Marketing's Relationship to Sales

I get so frustrated when I read job classifieds that advertise sales jobs disguised as marketing jobs. Marketing and sales are completely different functions. Or, at least, sales is one part of the marketing process. You can't have sales without marketing. But, you can have marketing without sales, especially if the marketing is poorly planned and executed.

Marketing develops and implements the strategy that generates interest in products resulting in leads for the sales force. You need to separate the two functions. You first need a marketing plan. Then, you need to sell your product to people who show an interest in or a need for your products and services.

But, it doesn't end there. A company's sales force provides important customer feedback to marketing. This includes favorable and unfavorable comments, experiences and attitudes about the product. Marketing uses this information to adjust their marketing plan.

## Your Marketing Budget

As a general rule, I set my monthly marketing budget at 5 to 7 percent of estimated sales. If I set my monthly sales goal at $4,000, my marketing budget is $200 to $300. But, I only use it if I need it. You don't have to spend every dollar you budget. But, there may be months when you need to spend more if you are in a slump. Learn how to stretch your budget.

## Learn from Your Peers

The good news is that many of the important marketing research activities described above have already been completed for you. You just need to know where to find the information. You need to put your pride aside and seek guidance and support from other personal chefs who have learned how to successfully market their business. If you join one of the personal chef associations, you will have access to more information than you will ever need.

By writing this book, I am sharing my experiences with you so that you will make one of two choices. Either you will determine that you have the skill sets and confidence to enter into this profession or you will throw your hands up in the air, turn around and walk away having saved a lot of aggravation, time and money.

## What We Already Know

Thanks to the hard work of a lot of people who have come before you, there is a lot of information that is already known about the personal chef industry. This information can be weaved into your marketing plan.

Because I understand marketing principles, I am able to give you a head start by summarizing what I believe are the key questions you need to have answered when determining how to market your business, including:

- Who could use a personal chef service?
- Who wants a personal chef service?
- Who needs a personal chef service?
- When do they need a personal chef service?
- How do you tell people about your business?
- How do you convert prospects to leads?
- How do you convert leads into clients?
- How do you keep clients?
- How do you get referrals from clients?

## Prospecting 101

A few years ago, I owned a business in the entertainment industry. Sales were lagging and I could sense the morale was down on my sales team. When this happens, sales people tend to stray from basic selling principles and try too hard to land the "big sale". So, I took three of my sales people to lunch at a very busy restaurant and asked them to look around the room and write down how many prospective clients they could identify that might be interested in our product.

I watched as they intently looked from table to table. When they spotted a prospect, they would quickly make a note and resume their search.

After about two minutes, I told them to stop. I asked each salesperson to tell me who they identified as a prospect and why. Each one identified five or six of the approximately sixty patrons as prospects. Two of the prospects were on each list.

Their reasons for picking their prospects involved only two senses – seeing and hearing. They primarily chose their prospects based on their physical appearance (well-dressed, well-groomed, smiling, etc...) or their voice.

They failed my test. I explained to them that every single person in that room was a prospect on some level. Personal appearance, size, hair color, skin color, age, and other physical characteristics cause us to discriminate when it comes to marketing and sales. This also holds true for geographic location, age, race and all of those factors that affect prejudice.

I didn't even tell you what we were selling because that isn't important. It's not important because everyone should be a considered to be a prospect for any product or service. They might know someone who needs your product or service. For example, you might not be in the market to purchase a jet engine. But, you might have an uncle who works in the purchasing department for an airplane manufacturer.

Would you approach a seven year old boy and tell him about your personal chef business? Probably not. However, I was doing a cooking demonstration at a kitchen appliance store. While the parents browsed the showroom, a little boy climbed up on a stool at the cooking island and asked what I was doing. I told him I was cooking and that I was a personal chef. He asked me what a personal chef was. So, I told him that if his mom or dad couldn't cook because they were too busy, I would come to his home and cook supper. That's all it took. He jumped down, ran to his parents and gave them the sales pitch for me. They signed on for my service as soon as their new kitchen renovation was complete.

The lesson is that everyone is a prospect for your personal chef business. Why? Every person must eat to stay alive. They, or someone they know, will have a need for your services either now or at some point in the future.

## It's All About Timing

I've received hundreds of letters from real estate companies who are interested in selling my house. There are agents that I receive information from every month or so. They have a marketing plan in place that keeps their name in front of me on a monthly basis. I am not interested in selling my house today. But, if I do decide to put it on the market, I have a short list of agents that I will interview because I've kept their information on file and appreciate their persistence.

Keeping your name in front of clients on a regular basis is known as, "Top of Mind Awareness."

## Who Needs It and When?

We also know that there are certain events in a person's life that "trigger" the buying cycle. This is true with any product. Catching a cold triggers the need to buy cough syrup or tissue. Changes in the seasons and weather initiate our purchase of certain types of clothing and accessories. The personal chef service is no different. Here is a list of reasons people might consider hiring a personal chef.

- Too busy to cook
- Physically disabled
- Just had surgery
- Had or will be having a new baby
- Wants to start a diet
- Ordered to eat healthier by doctor
- Kids are involved in activities
- Want more free time
- Single and can't cook
- Just married and don't know how to cook
- Tired of eating at restaurants
- Tired of carry out food
- Tired of pizza delivery
- Empty nesters
- Wants to give the service as a gift
- Throwing a party
- Guests are visiting from out of town
- Wants more "family time"
- Wants/Needs to save money

Look over the list above and think about how to deliver your message to people who are most likely to enter into the buying cycle in the near future.

There are recognizable triggers that enable you to focus your marketing efforts. Others are more obscure and require you to constantly keep your business in front of prospects so that they remember to contact you when the need arises.

### *Seasonal Triggers*

Do you recognize the seasonal triggers? There are certain professions that get very busy at certain times of the year. People involved in accounting and tax related fields are going to be busiest from January to mid-April.

When are people most likely to commit to a diet and eating healthier? January, of course!

Parents find it difficult to cook when their kids are involved in seasonal sports. Basketball, football, baseball and softball seasons, etc. You can market to these groups by advertising in their game programs, by sponsoring a team, or by speaking to an athletic booster organization.

People usually have parties around holidays like July 4th, Memorial Day, Christmas, Easter, Thanksgiving, birthdays, etc. And, what better gift is there for a man to give his wife or mother for Mothers Day, Sweetest Day, Valentines Day or just because she deserves a break!

## *Medical Triggers*

There are medical triggers. People undergo surgical procedures, give birth or are ordered to eat healthier for a variety of medical reasons. Doctors can be a great source of referrals.

## *Health and Fitness Triggers*

There are a lot of people out there who want to either maintain their health or improve their physical fitness. They belong to health clubs, gyms, cycling clubs, running clubs, racquetball and tennis clubs, and even weight loss support groups. These types of businesses and organizations are fertile ground for prospecting and lead development. Ask about advertising or sponsorship opportunities. Also, find out if they would allow you to put on a seminar or speak at an event as a service to their members.

## *Special Occasions*

Gift certificates are given for a variety of reasons. Real estate agents give gifts when their client purchases a home. Companies or coworkers give gifts to recognize performance or celebrate a personal achievement. Don't forget wedding anniversaries, religious occasions, house warmings, etc.

## Turning Prospects Into Leads

Now that you know what a prospect is, you need to focus on converting prospects into leads. A lead is someone who shows an interest in your product or service. I classify my leads as cold, warm and hot.

### Cold Lead

A cold lead is someone that could become a client sometime in the next six months. It could also be a referral that someone has given me. For example, my daughters are involved in school functions. Many of the activities occur around dinner time. When I attend one of those athletic events, musical programs or a practice, I know that if a parent is there, they are not at home cooking dinner. Therefore, I try to engage in some sort of conversation about my business and hand out business cards. They might have an interest or give me a referral. These are cold leads.

### Warm Lead

A cold lead becomes warm when someone indicates that they may have an interest and either says they will call me or they want me to call them. Their interest goes beyond telling me I have a "neat" or "cool" business.

### Hot Lead

A hot lead is a person that has a very strong interest in meeting and trying my service. I am very careful about who I move to this level. If the first question they ask is "How much does it cost?," I move on. If they say, "I'd like some more information about your business," and they agree to meet with me at their home, they are a hot lead. The chances of a hot lead becoming a client are greater than 90 percent.

## Conversion Tools

You must have the proper tools to convert a prospect into a lead. You can't just expect a stranger to walk up to you and, out of the blue, say "I bet you are a personal chef. I want to be one of your clients." Besides confidence, here are some of the tools you need.

### Elevator Speech

An "elevator speech" is a brief description of your business. It's called an elevator speech because you should be able to briefly explain your business to someone in the time it takes the elevator to move to the next floor. My elevator speech goes something like this...

*"Hi, my name is Brian and I am a personal chef. I can come into your home and cook up to a month's worth of healthy, delicious dinners that you can simply reheat, serve and eat at your convenience. And...I do the grocery shopping and clean your kitchen!"*

### Business Card

Your business card is the best advertising investment you can make. They aren't expensive to produce, especially if you have the ability to design and print them using your personal computer. If you don't have that ability, go to a local commercial printer or quick printer and ask for design help. You should include your name, your business name, logo, and telephone number. Your fax number, cellular phone number, E-mail address and web site address are all optional.

There are a lot of ways to use your business cards. When I am in networking mode, I follow the "three-foot rule." I often hand out at least two business cards to each person that comes within three feet of me. I ask the person to pass the extra cards to someone they know that might be able to use my service.

Using a tip from sales guru, author and trainer Tom Hopkins, I often write "Thank You" on the back of my card and tell them, "I am thanking you in advance for helping me spread the word about my business and the possibility of serving you in the future."

I also use business card magnets (available at most office supply stores). I use my magnetic business card to stick my client's menu on their refrigerator.

Another business card that I use is actually a postcard. I keep these in my van to hand out at special events or at more

informal social settings. I've even placed a small stack of these cards between the rear windshield wiper on the back of my van, just above my magnetic sign. I've done this while parked at the grocery store, a shopping mall or at one of my kid's sporting or school events. People do take them.

## Vehicle Signs

Another effective and economical way to promote your business is to turn your vehicle into a rolling billboard. I will attest,

*This is a 4.25"x5.5" postcard printed on red card stock. You get four on each sheet.*

as will most other personal chefs, that having your business name and contact information on your car or van will generate inquiries. People approach me in parking lots, leave notes on my windshield, and even call and leave a message that they were driving behind me and wrote down my telephone number.

## Paint Job or Magnetic Signs?

Getting a new paint scheme on your vehicle can be very expensive and can limit your ability to convert your vehicle back into an inconspicuous family vehicle if needed. Instead of painting the entire vehicle, some people have their logos painted on the windows or on decals. This can cost you anywhere between $50 for vinyl lettering to $3,000 for a complete graphics paint job.

I prefer to use magnetic signs. These signs are printed on heavy duty magnetic vinyl material. You can put one on each side of your vehicle (usually on the front doors) and one on the rear of your vehicle. It's important to make sure these signs are well-designed so that they are not too cluttered. You want people to be able to identify that you are a personal chef and to clearly read your telephone number. You can purchase a set of magnetic vehicle signs for as little as $75. Check on the Internet or in the yellow pages for local sign companies.

# Chapter 19
# *Finding Clients*

Once you organize your business, purchase your equipment and get your menu together, you need to find clients. I believe there are more clients out there than all of the personal chefs in the United States cooking 24/7 can handle. Just to give you an idea, there are approximately 80 million family households with three or more residents. If there are even 7,000 personal chefs, each one has a potential of 11,000 prospects if equally divided. And, while this is fertile profession, there are some important factors to consider.

## Location

Location is critical when establishing a retail business. It's no different for the personal chef industry. If you live in a thriving, metropolitan area, you will have no trouble finding clients if you put together a solid marketing plan. However, if you have to drive 30 miles to the closest grocery store or you reside in a community where the unemployment level is at an all time high, you might struggle a bit.

I am fortunate enough to reside in a north suburb of Indianapolis in one of the wealthiest counties in the United States. There is low unemployment. People have disposable income. And, there are a lot of two income and very busy families. It's easy finding clients where I live.

I do believe however, that if I opened a personal chef business in a little farming community 20 miles from my home, that I would still be successful. However, I would definitely have to work a lot harder to find and keep clients. Again, it's all about marketing.

## Networking

One of the best ways to find new clients is through referrals from family, friends, acquaintances or satisfied clients. Starting your own personal chef business is not like starting a multi-level marketing business selling soap, vitamins, skin care products or long distance. People aren't going to avoid you or refuse to answer your telephone calls and E-mails. So, do not be afraid to ask people that you know for a list of people they know that may need or enjoy your service.

Tap in to a variety of networking opportunities. Get involved in associations such as your local Chamber of Commerce, a business networking group or your church. Tell people what you do. They will be impressed and will tell others about you. Don't forget to give them a stack of business cards to hand out.

I am involved in my church and community theater. Both of these activities provide me with ample opportunities to prepare some great dishes for dinners, receptions, parties, fund-raisers and more. I always put a stack of recipe cards with my contact information next to my dish.

### Health & Medical Referrals

There are a lot of opportunities to get referrals from people involved in the health and medical professions. This can be an excellent source of referrals if you intend to offer healthy cooking options.

Post information about your business at local health clubs and provide information about your business to personal trainers, massage therapists, or nutrition consultants. They benefit by being able to offer their clients with additional health resources. You might also consider offering an incentive such as a small finders fee or a free dinner for any quality referrals that come your way. Always offer to reciprocate the referrals by giving information about their business to your clients.

Doctors are also a good referral source. I have received numerous referrals from physicians specializing in weight loss, diabetes, cancer, and other areas where nutrition is key to a patient's treatment or recovery. Another key medical referral source comes from the maternity sector. Contact local obstetricians, pediatricians, and birthing centers for permission to include your information in any publications or information packets for new or expecting mothers. New moms can definitely use your services and, if they know about your service far enough in advance, they can request your service as a gift from friends, family or coworkers.

### *Client Referrals*

One of my best sources for referrals are my satisfied clients. I always ask my clients to tell others about my service. If they make a referral and that client remains a client for three months, I reward them with a dinner party for eight people. It might be a backyard barbecue, a chili dinner, lasagna supper or even a tailgate party. It's a great way to let some of their friends or family meet you and sample your menu.

## Chapter 20

# *Time to Close the Sale*

If you thought you just had to hand out a few business cards and cook, you are in for a big surprise. Welcome to the wonderful world of sales.

The good news is that you don't have to be the stereotypical slimy salesperson. You have the advantage of selling a product that virtually sells itself. You don't have to be aggressive or a smooth talker. You just have to be able to ask a few questions and listen to your clients talk themselves into signing up for your service.

First, however, you need to schedule a sales call, also known as a client interview.

## Client Interviews (or Sales Presentation)

Before you ever agree to cook for a client, you need to do an in-home interview. I can't emphasize enough how important this is. There are a few reasons for meeting with a client and their family in their home.

First, your time is valuable and you don't want to waste it chasing business that will never happen. If a hot prospect agrees to take an hour of their time to let you come to their house, they are very interested and, in most instances, will hire you as their personal chef. I will not take anyone on as a client without meeting with them in their home. The only exception is when someone purchases a gift certificate. I will sometimes go ahead and schedule a cook date and hope that the person likes the service enough to sign on.

Another important reason to meet in their home is it allows you and your client to size each other up. I want my client to meet me and feel totally comfortable with me coming into their home, especially if they aren't going to be there when I cook. And, as I always tell my prospective clients, I want to make sure that I feel comfortable with them.

I also need to inspect the kitchen and cooking environment. I want to make sure that I know what types of appliances they have and explain to them what they need to do prior my arrival to make sure that I have enough work space and freezer space. I also inspect the kitchen for any type of damage and make note of it so that I know whether or not any damage was my fault or already existing.

## Setting Up the Meeting

Once a person calls me or E-mails me that they would like to know more about my services, I call them. The conversation is brief and I don't answer any specific questions over the telephone. Again, if they focus on cost I don't even offer to set up a meeting. I simply ask them, "Is price your primary concern?" If so, I am probably not going to be able to help them. My best, long-term clients are concerned about saving time, eating healthier or reducing stress.

If they don't ask about price, I attempt to schedule an appointment. My pitch goes something like this:

*"I'm glad you called me. It sounds like you could really use a personal chef. Before I agree to take you on as a client, I need to schedule about an hour to meet with you and your family so that I can answer any questions and complete a nutritional profile for each person who will be eating these meals. Also, I think it's important that we get to meet each other so that you feel comfortable with me coming into your home and I feel comfortable being in your home."*

I then give them a choice of times to meet. NEVER ever ask, "Would you like to schedule a meeting?" If you give them an out, they'll take it. I simply ask, "Which evening next week is better for you, Tuesday or Wednesday?" Whatever night they pick, I give them two time options, either at 6:00 or 8:00. This gives me time to conduct an hour meeting and then get to my next appointment if I can schedule another.

How well does this work? I get appointments with about 80 percent of my "hot" leads.

## Important Opening Question

After arriving at the client's house, I like to make sure that all available family members are sitting around the kitchen table. I write down their names, in clockwise order, on my client profile form so that I don't forget who they are. Then, I put my pen and paper to the side, lean forward and say...

*"Tell me, why do you believe a personal chef, like me, can help your family at this point in time?"*

I shut up and listen. If nobody says anything, I just sit there and wait until someone answers. They will.

You already know, from the reasons I talked about earlier, why you are there. But, you want the customer to reiterate their problem so that you can be "the solution."

They usually give me a reason like, "We are so busy and are tired of eating fast food." I don't respond. Let them break the silence by coming up with another reason. They might add, "I need to lower my cholesterol and lose about ten pounds."

As long as you remain quiet, they will come up with more reasons. When they run out of reasons, they will tell you.

I then summarize their problems and ask another question. "Let me see if I understand. Your life is hectic. You don't have time to cook healthy meals for your family. You want to address some weight and health issues. And, you want to have more time around the kitchen table with your family. Did I forget, anything?" They will usually not add anything else and say, "That's right."

I then say, "Those are all excellent reasons. I can help you address some of those issues."

Now, I go through my menu, meal plans and pricing, being sure to answer any questions they might have.

I then ask, "Which schedule best meets your needs, bi-weekly or monthly?" We then discuss what type of schedule works best.

## Getting Them to Commit (Asking for the Order)

I then open my day planner and ask, "Which day of the week works best for you?" At this point, they will usually give you a day. I always ask what their second choice is.

Here's where you have to be confident and bold. You need to ask for the order without actually "asking" for the order. This is called an "assumptive" close.  I say something like, "While you get your checkbook or credit card information, I'll look over my schedule and set your first cook date. Then, I'll ask each of you about your likes, dislikes, food allergies and other information and we can go over some specifics regarding the cook day, itself."

You should know that in three years as a personal chef, I have never had anyone stop me at this point and back out.

## Negotiating

There will be times when a prospective client tries to negotiate for a lower price. Absolutely, positively do not play this game. If you negotiate and give them a lower price, they will brag to all of their friends on the great deal you gave them. You'll soon have everyone asking you for the "same deal" you gave to your other clients. When people try to negotiate, I simply tell them, "I would love to be able to offer you a discount but I would have to compromise on the quality of your meals to maintain my profit margin and I don't want to get a reputation for substituting quality for price." If you take this approach, they can't and won't argue. If they still attempt to negotiate, simply tell them that your price is firm, apologize for taking up their time, and leave. Either they'll stop you and sign up for your service or they'll let you walk.

## Client Profile

Once I get the commitment, I then proceed with completing the client profile. There's no point in doing this if they don't want to sign up for the service. I gather basic information about the family, their likes and dislikes, tolerance to spicy foods, and more. The form I use is on the opposite page.

### When It Doesn't Work

Out of every fifteen meetings, I will have one that does not result in an actual sale. One time, the people weren't home when I arrived and they did not reschedule. One said that they wanted to "talk it over" and they'd get back to me (I never heard from them again). And the rest just aren't going to buy. Based on their body language, personality and focus on cost, I did not even try to close the sale. I am a pretty good judge of character and I go with my gut instincts. I didn't feel like these people would be good clients, even if they did sign on. So, I walked.

**DOCTOR DINNER**

### Customer Record Card

Customer Name: _____

Address: _____

_____

Telephone Number: _____

Emergency Number(s): _____

Entry Information: _____

Pet Information: _____

Family Members: _____

_____

**FOOD INFORMATION**

| Dislikes | | Allergies | Needs |
|---|---|---|---|
| _____ | _____ | _____ | ☐ Low Fat    ☐ Low Calorie |
| _____ | _____ | _____ | ☐ Low Salt   ☐ Diabetic |
| _____ | _____ | _____ | ☐ Other |
| _____ | _____ | _____ | _____ |

Spice Scale: 1 2 3 4 5 6 7 8 9 10

**SERVICE INFORMATION**

☐ Bi-Weekly    ☐ 5x2    ☐ 10x1    Adult___    Teen___    Child___

☐ Monthly      ☐ 5x4    ☐ 10x2    Adult___    Teen___    Child___

TOTAL COST_____

**Payment Information**

☐ Check    ☐ Visa    ☐ Master Card

Acct. No. ☐☐☐☐ ☐☐☐☐ ☐☐☐☐ ☐☐☐☐  Exp: __/__

**Doctor Dinner**

*Personal Chef Service*

In these instances, I simply say, "I sense that you have some hesitation or concerns – and that's okay. I don't want you to feel obligated to hire me. You've got all of my contact information. Why don't you think it over and let me know in the next couple of days how you would like to proceed?" Both of these people were kind enough to send me a nice E-mail and say that they were going to "pass" and they'd keep me in mind and refer others to my business.

## Surviving Slumps

Every salesperson experiences slumps. Sales is a numbers game and you are playing to a law of averages. Some slumps are short-lived. Others can last for days, weeks or months. You may slump every other week. Or, you may go a whole year without experiencing a slump.

I consider myself in a slump if I have two weeks in a row without a single cook date, one month without an inquiry, or two months without signing a new client. Any one of these factors causes me to shift my marketing activities into overdrive.

Slumps can be caused by outside stimuli that you can't control such as the economy, weather, world affairs (such as September 11th), and so on. But, most slumps are self-induced. It's easy to become complacent during those times when business is booming. That's when undisciplined salespeople get too cocky. I know, I've done it myself, I've spent days on the golf course or lounging by the swimming pool when I should have been selling. I've also gone on spending sprees because I had some extra cash. When the slumps hit, and they will, you need to minimize their sting by having qualified leads in the queue and money in the bank. Nothing lights a fire under me faster that looking at my schedule four weeks out and realizing I don't have any client's scheduled or cash flow in my pipeline.

Just prior to becoming a personal chef, I took a sales job at a local winery. Over those three months, I didn't close one sale.

This was the worst sales slump I had ever been in. But, it wasn't my fault. The business manager/co-owner had taken a "professional" sales course and thought that "her way" was the only way to sell her products. It was my job to sell meeting space and special events. The meeting space was very unique, had a great ambiance and, in my opinion, would be easy to sell. However, she imposed her selling methodology on me and tried to get me to forget everything I had learned in 30 years of selling. I did not make one sale in three months. My confidence was shattered and I really had doubts about my ability to sell. It took re-reading my sales books and listening to sales and motivational tapes to get back into my groove.

Since becoming a personal chef, I have been successful in my sales efforts. I closed every single one of my first 17 sales. That means that I walked out of their house with a cook day scheduled and a deposit in my hand. I then hit a small slump. I lost my next three sales. Today, I close about 9 out of 10 sales.

The winery I worked for went out of business.

## Chapter 21

# *Show Me the Money*

You are offering a unique service whereby you can establish your policies and communicate those policies to your clients up front. Collecting payment has never been a problem for me.

## Payment Up Front

My policy is simple. The client pays for the service in advance or I don't cook. I explain that it is important for me to have the money in the bank so that I can purchase their groceries and other supplies. When a customer first signs up for the service at the client interview, I collect payment for the first cook date that I try to schedule within the next 5 to 10 days. If they refuse to make that initial payment, it's almost certain they are not going to sign up for the service and I head for the door. On each cook day, I leave an invoice for the next cook date.

### *Paying by Check*

If paying by check, I must receive their payment at least five days prior to the scheduled cook day. Some prefer to pay one cook day in advance. That's how most personal chefs like to handle the payment process, as well.

### Credit Cards Increase Sales

I believe that to succeed in business today, you have to offer your clients a variety of payment options. Besides the convenience, many of my clients choose to pay by credit card because they earn perks offered by their bank or credit card company. One of my clients is actually a corporate sales representative for one of the "major" credit card companies. I don't mind paying the small fee to be able to accept credit cards because I know it increases my sales.

If they pay by credit card, I take down their card information and process their payment about a week in advance so that the funds are deposited into my business checking account a day or two before the cook day. I always contact my client by phone or E-mail to let them know that their payment is being processed.

## Cancellations

Besides collecting payment for cooking services, I also charge for last-minute cancellations. I require at least five days notice for cancellation. I do make exceptions for illness or emergency situations. However, if a client just gets "too busy" to submit their menu, which happens on occasion, and they want to reschedule, I charge a $50 cancellation and rescheduling fee. If I show up at their house with a van full of groceries and they aren't there and forgot to call me to cancel (this has happened) I will invoice them. I include this tidbit of information on my client policy sheet.

# Chapter 22

# *Shopping*

Shopping is important to your personal chef business in many ways. If you include the cost of groceries in the price of your service, it only makes sense that for each dollar you save, you add a dollar to your profit margin. Also, you don't want to spend one more minute in the grocery store than needed. Your shopping goals are to save money and save time.

## Fresh Ingredients

You want to make sure that you use the freshest ingredients available. Summers are ideal because you can shop for fresh vegetables and herbs at farmers markets, roadside fruit and vegetable stands, or grow your own vegetables and herbs.

The supermarket I shop at usually carries excellent produce, seafood and meat. However, Monday morning is usually the worst time to shop because fresh items usually get picked over on the weekends. At 7:00 a.m., they usually haven't had a chance to replenish the produce and put fresh seafood and meat products out yet. If I know in advance that I need something special for Monday morning, I will call the produce or meat department managers or stop by and give them a list of things I need to have set aside for my Monday morning shopping excursion. They are more than happy to accommodate me and will have everything ready for me.

I look for the freshest vegetables and inspect the seafood and meat visually and by smelling it. If it's not fresh, I will tell the manager. If they don't have fresh items in the stock room, I will either make a substitution or go to another store. I ask the manager to call ahead to their other local stores to see if they have the product on hand.

Depending on the dish I am preparing, I may use frozen vegetables if fresh vegetables are not available or out of season.

## Packaged Ingredients

While some personal chefs get involved in making fresh marinara, salsa, and other ingredients, I do use some canned or prepackaged items. This includes pasta, tomato sauce, and other items that do not need to be homemade. Primarily, these are things that I can purchase in bulk at a wholesale club or at my local supermarket.  It also includes ground beef, sausage, or other meat and dairy products that I can freeze or that have a long shelf life. If I know that I have four or five cook days in one week and there is a special on ground beef on the weekend, I will purchase what I need and freeze it.  Again, I do try to use ingredients as soon as possible.

## Getting to Know Store Managers and Employees

I can't stress how important it is to get to know the people that work at the store where you shop. Introduce yourself to the store manager, the produce manager, the bakery manager, the meat and seafood managers, the cashiers and the sackers. I even know the night shift stocking crew because they are always finishing up stocking the shelves when I arrive in the morning and they always help me locate items that I can't find. Introduce yourself to all of these very important people on your first shopping day. Give them business cards and a brochure. Tell them that you would appreciate knowing about any sales specials, new items, or information about pending product shortages, recalls or price increases.

They need to know who you are because you will be one of their biggest customers when your business shifts into high gear. When cooking full time, I can easily spend an average of $1,000 or more per week. They will go out of their way to help you if you are spending that kind of money at their store. They will also tell others about your business and become an extension of your sales force.

I always try to go to the same cashier when I check out. She knows what I do and that I am in a hurry. Because she knows my routine, she even has noticed when I've forgotten something. She also makes sure that I take advantage of coupons and special promotions. And, as I am walking out the door, I often hear her telling the next people in line that I am a personal chef and explains how my business works. You can't buy that kind of publicity! The sackers know how I want my groceries sacked and what items to put together. When I have a lot of bags, they wheel them out and help me load them into my van. This is a big help.

## Map Out Your Store

I spent one morning walking through the supermarket mapping out where items are located. I then created a shopping list of the most frequently purchased items in order of how I travel through the store. I go through the produce department first, bakery second, seafood and meat, wine, international items, soups, baking goods, spices, etc.

## Shopping List

While I now have my list in a spreadsheet on my computer, I recommend that you do something similar to what I have created. When I go through my client's menu and the recipes, I highlight the items I need to purchase. I then go through my in-home inventory and circle the items that I have on hand

and don't have to purchase. Always shop at home first. Then, when I go through the supermarket, I pick up only what I absolutely need and check off those items that I put in my shopping cart. I always review my list just before I go through the checkout lane.

*Items on my shopping list are in order of how I move through the store. This allows me to save time hunting for items or having to back track.*

**Vegetables**
- Tomatoes
- Cherry Tomatoes
- Garlic
- Yellow Onion
- Red Onion
- Potatoes
- Red Potatoes
- Baking Potatoes
- Yellow Potatoes
- Sweet Potatoes
- Green Beans
- Broccoli
- Sliced Carrots
- Baby Carrots
- Sliced Mushrooms
- Whole Mushrooms
- Portabella
- Celery
- Red Pepper
- Green Pepper
- Asparagus
- Zucchini
- Yellow Squash
- Egg Plant
- Pine Nuts
- Lettuce
- Cabbage
- Red Cabbage
- Spinach
- Salad In a Bag
- _____

**Fruit**
- Lemons
- Limes
- Oranges
- Apples
- _____

**Fish**
- Tuna Steaks
- Salmon
- Crab Meat
- Shrimp
- Orange Roughy

**Meat**
- Chicken Breasts
- Chicken Thighs
- Chicken Legs
- Chicken Wings
- Whole Chicken
- Turkey Breast
- Veal Scallopini
- Veal Chops
- Beef Tenderloin
- Filet Mignon
- Ground Turkey
- Ground Beef
- Ground Chuck

- Sirloin
- Round Steak
- Ribeye Steak
- Chuck Roast
- Rump Roast
- Cube Steak
- Pork Tenderloin
- Pork Chops
- Baby Back Ribs
- Spare Ribs
- Whole Chicken
- Turkey Tenders
- Chopped Ham
- Ham Steaks
- Whole Ham
- Sausage
- Italian Sausage
- Bacon
- _____

**Wine**
- Red
- White
- Marsala
- Sherry
- _____

**Italian**
- Spaghetti Sauce
- Marinara Sauce
- Alfredo Sauce
- Spaghetti
- Angel Hair Pasta
- Lasagna Noodles
- Fine Noodles
- Egg Noodles

**Mexican**
- Tortilla
- Fajita Seasoning
- Taco Seasoning
- Taco Sauce
- Green Taco Sauce
- Spanish Rice
- _____

**Oriental**
- Soy Sauce
- Water Chestnuts
- Sprouts
- Rice
- Hoisin Sauce
- _____

**Canned Meat**
- Chunk Chicken
- Whole Chicken
- Tuna
- Salmon
- Clams
- Clam Juice

- _____

**Soup**
- Cream of Chicken
- Cream of Celery
- Cream of Mushroom
- Cream of Shrimp
- Beef Broth
- Chicken Broth
- Chicken Stock
- _____

**Baking**
- Flour
- Sugar
- Brown Sugar
- Corn Meal
- Bisquick
- Coconut
- _____

**Spices & Oil**
- Olive Oil
- Vegetable Oil
- Canola Oil
- Sesame Oil
- _____

**Nuts & Dried Fruit**
- Slivered Almonds
- Walnut Pieces
- Pecan Pieces
- Raisins
- Apricots
- Prunes
- Currants

**Canned Vegetables**
- Green Beans
- Peas
- Corn
- Carrots
- _____

**Stuffing**
- Stuffing

**Tomato Products**
- Tomato Sauce
- Tomato Paste
- Diced Tomatoes
- Stewed Tomatoes
- Italian Tomatoes
- Mexican Tomatoes
- Pizza Sauce
- _____

**Condiments**
- Ketchup
- Mustard

- Brown Mustard
- BBQ Sauce
- Mayonnaise
- Green Olives
- Black Olives
- Capers
- _____

**Jelly & Jams**
- Apple Jelly
- Peach Preserves

**Salad Dressing**
- Mayo
- Ranch
- French
- Blue Cheese
- Italian
- Raspberry V.

**Dairy**
- Ricotta
- Sour Cream
- Cottage Cheese
- Heavy Cream
- Half & Half
- Milk
- Eggs
- Mozzarella
- Parmesan
- Cheddar
- Velveeta
- Monterey Jack
- Taco Cheese
- Cream Cheese
- Butter
- Margarine
- Pizza Crust
- Bread Dough
- Pie Crust
- Yeast

**Frozen Foods**
- Green Beans
- Peas
- Corn
- Spinach
- Corn on the Cobb
- Mixed Vegetables
- Raspberries
- Hash Browns
- Shrimp

**Paper**
- Gladware
- Ovenware
- Freezer Bags
- Plastic Wrap
- Aluminum Foil

## Chapter 23

# *Diary of A Personal Chef*

## Preparing for a Cook Day

Every cook day is different and can be full of surprises if you don't have a plan. My goal is to start my cook day the night before so that I don't have to rush around getting everything together early in the morning.

### *Doing Laundry*

I always make sure that I have clean towels, dish rags, apron, chef's coat and hat. If I need to, I do a load of laundry. Okay, my wife does my laundry. But, it's up to me to make sure I have put my dirty stuff in the laundry room. It's important to treat the stains, use bleach and starch your apron, coat and hat if they need it. You want to look your best.

### *Making My Shopping List*

I print out my client's menu and any recipes that I am unfamiliar with so that I can put together my shopping list. As I mentioned earlier, I have a printed shopping list that is organized according to the store layout. This makes it much easier and allows me to cut down on my shopping time in the morning.

### Checking Inventory

Because I try to purchase some staple items like spices, tomato sauce, baking ingredients and pasta in bulk, I shop my own inventory first so that I don't have to purchase items that I already have on hand. This really helps profitability. I also usually have extra produce such as potatoes, onions, garlic, carrots and celery on hand. I gather my inventory items together, bag them and put them by the door. I put any cold items in my freezer/refrigerator in the garage.

### Generating Labels, Menus and Invoices

One of the last tasks is to print out labels for the containers, a clean menu that I post on the clients refrigerator, and an invoice for the next cook date. I put these in my client's folder that I carry with me on the cook day. The folder contains information such as the client profile, emergency telephone numbers, entry instructions, special recipes and more.

## The Cook Day

### Early Morning System Check

It's always good to go over the menu and shopping list one last time to make sure you haven't forgotten anything. It's very frustrating to discover two hours into cooking that you forgot a key ingredient. You have to shut down the ovens, turn off the burners, and truck off to the grocery store. It disrupts your work flow and can add as much as an extra hour or two to your cook day, especially if there isn't a store close by.

Now is a good time to mention that I like to take an inventory of my client's pantry, freezer and refrigerator during my initial consultation and again when I arrive to cook just in case I forget an item or run out of an ingredient such as brown sugar, olive oil or even a can of mushroom soup. I always leave a note if I use something of the client's. I either reimburse them or replace the item as soon as possible, even if it means making a trip back to their house later that day.

I pack up my mini van, always making sure that I put items in the same place each time. My cookware duffle bag, portable pantry, cleaning supplies and clothing have their special place. I take a visual inventory of my van to make sure I have everything.

## Shopping We Will Go

It's off to the grocery store. I try to arrive between 7:15 and 7:30. If I arrive any earlier, the fresh produce, seafood and meats aren't put out yet. I carry my shopping list and a copy of the menu. I put a check mark beside shopping list items as I put them in the cart and cross off each menu item when I have picked up all of the required ingredients. This is my check and balance to make sure I don't forget anything.

Again, I can't stress the importance of touching, squeezing, smelling and visually examining produce, seafood and meats to make sure they are of the highest quality. Also, check the expiration date of any dairy products or other perishable food items. I once emptied a quart of milk into a recipe only to end up with a lumpy, stinky mess. The milk had expired the week before. Besides having to throw out the dish I was making, I nearly got sick. It wasn't a pleasant experience and was a tough lesson learned.

## Arriving On Time

Once I arrive at the client's house, usually around 8:30 a.m., I take in my cleaning supplies and client folder. I turn on the oven and sanitize the work space including the counter tops, sinks, cook top and the inside of the microwave. I also sweep and mop the floor if they need it – especially if the client has pets. I even bring my own anti-bacterial hand soap that I put next to the sink so I can wash my hands frequently.

Library Resource Center
Renton Technical College
3000 N.E. 4th St.
Renton, WA 98056

After the work area is cleaned and prepped, I carry in the groceries, unpack the items and organize them. I put the produce items that need prepped by the sink. Canned goods go together on the counter. Spices and baking items go together. And I put meat, seafood and dairy products in either the refrigerator or in a cooler chest filled with ice, if refrigerator space is limited.

After I unpack the groceries and organize the kitchen, I unpack my cutting board, knives and utensils.

### Dress to Cook

I then put my chef's coat and apron on as well as my front and side towels. I dampen a cloth towel and hook under my tie-string in the front of my apron. This comes in handy if I have to quickly wipe something off my hands or wipe up a spill so that it doesn't harden on the counter top or stove. I hook my side towel under the apron string on my right hip so that I can use it to grab hot lids, pans, baking sheets or other hot items. I also use it to dry my hands when they get wet. Be careful, though, if your side towel is damp, don't grab hot items or you will burn yourself as the heat will quickly transfer through the damp towel.

### Prep Time

Next, I wash and prep my vegetables and put them into containers. I have plastic containers for sliced onions, chopped onions, minced onions, tomatoes, carrots, garlic, potatoes, squash, broccoli and whatever type of vegetable I need for my recipes. Having these items prepared saves a lot of time and makes cleanup easier at the end of the day.

I then do the same with meats. I cube beef, make pork medallions, cut up chicken, butterfly pork chops, filet fish, and so on. I always clean and disinfect my cutting boards and knives after cutting each meat product so there is minimal chance of contamination. I put the cut meat products into

Library Resource Center
Renton Technical College
3000 N.E. 4th St.
Renton, WA 98056

---

individual containers and back into the refrigerator until I need them.

## Let's Cook

I then begin to cook. I always start with the recipes that need the longest preparation and cook time. This includes anything that requires marinating, chilling or baking. This allows me to prepare quick side dishes, vegetables, sauces and other recipes that require minimal preparation and cook time in between.

While I have memorized many of my recipes, I still take them with me. Some personal chefs use recipe cards, recipe binders or printed recipe sheets. I recently started using my laptop computer. This cuts down on the paper and allows me to quickly pull up recipes, find ingredient substitutions, convert measurements or adjust recipes based on the number of servings. If you do decide to use a laptop computer, I highly recommend covering the keyboard portion in plastic wrap to avoid getting the keys wet or crusty. I always put the computer on a counter or table away from the sink or stove so that moisture or heat won't damage it.

## Labeling & Storing

After following proper cooling and packaging procedures, I label the containers and pack the items in the freezer, putting entrees on one shelf and side items on another. This makes it easier for the client to locate items.

## Cleaning Up

Cleaning up is the only part of this job I could do without. However, it's also one of the main reasons I get repeat business. My clients like coming home to a clean kitchen that smells great.

I bag up any trash and put it in trash receptacles either in the garage or outside. I then pack away any spices or other items that don't require washing. I hand wash my own cookware and utensils first so that I can pack them away and take them to my van.

Once the kitchen is cleared of anything that I brought, I wash any of my clients items that I used, such as baking dishes, utensils, silverware, glasses and broiling pans. I dry them and put them away in their proper places. I clean the work surfaces such as the counter tops, cook top, oven, microwave, refrigerator surface, cabinets, sink and faucets.

Next, I clean the kitchen floor. I use a broom to sweep the floors and then I use either a damp mop or my handy dandy Swiffer WetJet (what a great invention). Just make sure that you know what type of cleaners to use on all counter tops and floors.

And finally, I disinfect the counters and work surfaces. I gather my towels and any other items, lock the door and head for home, stopping by the bank if I need to make a deposit. I am usually home by the time my kids arrive home from school.

### Tending to Business

But, my day is not over. I spend the next hour or so checking E-mails for messages from clients or for new inquiries. I do my paperwork, accounting and any online banking.

That's my day. Other personal chefs' routines may vary, but not by much.

# Chapter 24

# *Moving Forward*

So, now that you've hopefully learned a few things about the personal chef industry, you need to decide what to do next.

I will tell you most personal chefs, especially those that have been at this for a long time, don't want you in this industry if you aren't going to have a positive impact. There are a lot of personal chefs that have no idea what they are doing. If the public has a bad experience with a personal chef, the industry can suffer. You don't want to be the cook that spoils the soup, so to speak.

You've probably heard the expression, "Bad news travels fast." In business, it's been called the "3/30 Rule". If someone has a good business experience, they usually tell three people. But, if that experience is bad, they will tell 30 people. Think about the last time you experienced bad customer service or had a bad retail experience. You probably told as many people as you could. It's just our nature. Who knows why?

Don't just rely on the information and advice in this book. While I've tried to provide you with the plain and simple truth about the personal chef industry and shared my experience and advice from other personal chefs, you need to do your homework.

When you have discerned that you have all of the information you need and possess the skill set to get started, then I say, "Go for it!"

You will have successes and you will have failures. Seek the guidance of other personal chefs, small business owners, and business consultants. You need to read cooking and business-related books, magazine articles, and information available on the Internet as often as possible. Most importantly, have confidence and develop a sense of humor.

And, finally, you can do what I do. Turn to God for help and guidance in times of despair and remember to give Him thanks for the many blessings He bestows.

## Chapter 25

# *Survival Tips from Other Personal Chefs*

To finish writing this book, I wanted to provide different perspectives from other personal chefs who are in various stages of business development. Some have just started. Some have been at in only for a couple of years. Others have been at this business for a long time. I asked them to answer this one question.

*"What advice would you give to a new personal chef for surviving their first 90 days in business?"*

Here are their responses.

"Don't quit your day job...just kidding. I think the first 90 days were my easiest. I was pumped up, full of you-know-what and vinegar. Everything seemed to go my way. It's after that initial burst of energy wears off that things get sketchy. Years ago, my father told me three things that have a daily impact on my desire and ability to pursue my business goals. First (I use this one to remind myself why I do this), "what would you do if money was no object?" Second, "make a plan, then work your plan" (another great reminder when I have one of those days that won't end). And third, "a successful man is marked by how well he handles Plan B." There's more, but that's about 2-cents' worth."

**Lynch Orr**
**Stone Soup, PCS**
**Nashville, TN**

"If you've asked and answered those hard, honest questions, and you've taken the jump to become a Personal Chef, quit the day job. What you might regard as "security" is in fact an anchor. The broadest leap in life is the leap of faith, but not taking it will doom you to stay put."

**Kent McDonald**
**Kent Cooks**
**Alexandria, VA**

Don't "dabble" at being a Personal Chef. Once you're trained, quit your day job and get cooking! Success comes only from experience. If you haven't already, spend a large part of your first 90 days marketing and advertising to get your name and services "out there". Don't tell your first client they're first - act like you've been doing this for years.

**Kenneth Hulme**
**The Portable Gourmet**
**Prescott, AZ**

"Well begun is half-done"—that sums up my advice. The more you prepare—for the client interview, your cook dates, your materials, your time line, and the actual cooking—the better the end result.

**Christine Schnee**
**Homemade**
**St. Louis, MO**

"Keep the faith and talk to other personal chefs for support. My first three months as a Personal Chef were the scariest, loneliest and most exciting three months I've had as a working adult. I was still working full time as an accountant during those three months. I consider the first three months of my business to be the first three months I started advertising and telling everyone that I was a pc. Because I was unhappy working as an accountant, I desperately wanted my business to take off so I could quit. I cooked only once in those first three months so I was simultaneously thrilled and disappointed. After much soul searching I came to the conclusion that I couldn't devote the time necessary to organizing and marketing my business while still working full time but I also needed to pay my bills. Fortunately, I worked for an awesome boss who was very understanding of my situation when I explained it to her and who agreed to let me "quit" my job as an employee (and thereby bound by the company rules of having to be in the office 8-5 M-F) and come back as a contractor working whatever hours I needed to complete my assignments. This has been a mixed blessing. On the one hand, I can set my own schedule taking days off to cook or the afternoon off to test recipes but it also means that I can't cook five days a week. I have a nest egg that I could tap if need be but for right now I'm going to try and swing both jobs as long as the office is understanding of my schedule. So for right now I guess I'm a "part time" pc and a "part time " accountant. Tenacity pays off and when you book that first gig you'll know instantly why you got into this business!."

**Cindi Billington**
**Gourmet On The Go**
**Collinsville, OK**


The first 90 days weren't the problem; it was the all the days (and months) after that up until 4 months ago that were the real problem! I officially launched in December 2001 but didn't get a paying client until January of 2002. I was anticipating being fully booked by March 2002; ha! I wasn't even fully booked by March 2003... My advice?  Hang in there! Don't give up! And most importantly, remember that your experience is going to be different from someone else's. I remember getting REALLY depressed reading how some chefs—especially you Brian! -- were fully booked with a waiting list after just a couple of months in business. I'm finally there, but it's taken 2 years. And knowing how fickle clients can be, I know that I can be looking again for new clients at any time.  As the president of the local chapter, I get a lot of calls from people wanting to get into the business. I'm very honest with them and tell them not to expect to make much in the first 2 years. Sure, it can be done, but I think it's more the exception than the rule. I went over a year with just one regular client; all the rest were one-offs or gift certificates. Fortunately I got great feedback from everyone; it was just a matter of them not being able to afford the service on a long-term basis.

**Betsy Rogers**
**Ovens To Betsy**
**Seattle, WA**


"My advice for surviving the first 3 years (not 90 days) is to listen to your own inner voice and follow your own gut instincts. Do not let people who are in different geographic regions, different economic zones and different lifestyles try to persuade you to do something you don't feel is right. Take advice and learn what you can from those that have successful PC businesses; especially from those in your own geographic area. Also, make your own business plan being as realistic as you believe is possible and remember to review your business plan often and amend it when it becomes necessary. Know that your business can be seasonal and plan vacations or time away during the slow months. Take lots of vitamins and get lots of sleep during the busy time. I started my business in 1999 and, although was told by everyone to "quit" my day job, I didn't.  I am glad I stuck to my guns and did what I felt was right. I am single and had no other source of income. Had I quit my day job back then, I would likely have lost my home. Another chef that I took the Personal Chef course with did quit his job. Nine months later he had to wait tables so he didn't lose his house. I was a part time pc for 3 years and only quit my "day job" when I felt financially secure enough. Plus I had built up my client base so that I was confident I would be working a minimum of 3 days a week if not more. Most weeks now I work 5+ days. When I was in University and took business I was told that 2 out of 3 business's fail within the first 3 years. I'm now in my 5th year of business and running a very successful business. I attribute this to doing things the way I felt was right and not by being influenced by others, especially those that weren't doing this for a living. "

**Robyn Goorevitch**
**Dining In Chez Vous**
**Toronto, Ontario**

"My advice is don't say "yes" to everything. I've been in business for a little over a year. In the beginning, I had requests to come in to cook only 2 or 3 meals, cook dinner for the same client every day, do a one time party for someone on a Saturday night and to provide a full service but drop my price. I politely declined all these offers. It wasn't what I'd worked out in my business plan and I wasn't going to alter my model for the sake of getting a little work. The end result? I'm booked with lots of clients and very profitable to boot. If you're confident about your plan, don't say yes to something that doesn't work for you."

**Mary Kernan**
**Homemade Today**
**Lexington, MA**

"Anytime I am approached by anyone thinking of entering the personal chef industry, I give them advice that I actually lived by. I advise that you need to save a nest egg. That nest egg should have enough money to pay all your bills for 6 months as well as 6 months for medical insurance if you do not have a spouse to cover you. Also it should include enough money for advertising. I researched where I wanted to advertised, found out the cost and included those amounts in my nest egg. I purchased any additional equipment I thought I might need while I still had my full time job. I also saved enough money to pay for the USPCA course in cash so I would not start my business in debt! Yes, this took me a year and a half to save, but it was the best thing I ever did because clients do not knock on your door in the beginning and I had to still pay my bills!"

**Nancy Ricks**
**Home Sweet Home**
**Jacksonville, FL**

"I agree with my fellow PC's, especially the 6 month nest egg and listening to your inner voice. Everyone has a unique situation and should "think outside the box" as to what would work for your business. The USPCA offers an outline for a typical or traditional Personal Chef business which doesn't work for the area I live in or my personality. I've also started this year to stock kitchens before people arrive for vacations or the season. This helps with the cash flow. Every year it seems I can think of another service that is needed here. The old saying "Find a need..." If the traditional meal replacement is not filling up your calendar, think of a different way to utilize your business. "

**Nancy Tracy**
**The Silver Chef**
**Sanibel, FL**

"I took the USPCA training in June, with the goal of starting up my business by October 1$^{st}$, keeping my part time "day job," and aiming at having 4 regular clients by the end of the year (at which time I was planning to quit the part time job). To date, I have had seven cook dates (several repeats) and now have three clients whom I will cook for once a month. Have given my notice and am hopeful to reach my goal by the end of the year. I'd say to be prepared for the hard work, like schleping equipment and groceries, standing on your feet for 5-6 hours, hauling everything back to the car, unloading and then dealing with getting dinner on your own table. I thoroughly enjoy what I'm doing, and I'm used to hard work, but I am wiped at the end of a cook day! Be a personal chef for your own family so you can relax when you get home at the end of a cook day!

**Mary Molish**
**No Plates Like Home**

"I recommend new chefs that call to ask about this profession- hang on to a regular income as long as they can. This is not an overnight success story. I support myself entirely on personal cheffing - I always thought I'd cook 5 days a week - but to be honest, I make a better salary now than I did wearing a suit into a hospital executive office every day. I try to cook 4 days a week with an office day (very important to keep up on paperwork and have time for new client interviews). Some full time chefs can do it 3 days a week plus an occasional pick up - so look carefully at your hourly wage (considering tax benefits) before you leave your blanket behind!"

**Laura Cotton**
**Baltimore, MD**

"People starting a personal chef business usually love to cook, but most everyone I mentored forgot it's a business. And like any other business you need a plan, you need to know what you want from it, and how you will define success. If you're not familiar with running a business you need to do your homework before you start, and that means talking, listening, reading, studying, and practicing. In my area the ones who succeed are the ones who participate in the chapter and/or spend time on the boards learning and sharing with other personal chefs. We are blessed to be in a sharing community here, so I always suggest new starters join the community of their choice, but join it and participate in it. "

**Judi Eidam**
**Dinners By Design**

**Sacramento, CA**

# Appendix A

# *Miscellaneous Resources*

## Personal Chef Associations & Organizations

**American Personal Chef Association**
4572 Delaware Street
San Diego, CA 92116
800-644-8389
619-294-2436
**www.personalchef.com**

**Personal Chefs Network**
P.O. Box 130692
The Woodlands, Texas 77393-0692
**www.personalchefsnetwork.com**
**877-905-CHEF**

**United States Personal Chef Association**
**(also Australian Personal Chef and Canadian Personal Chef Association)**
481 Rio Rancho Boulevard NE
Rio Rancho, New Mexico 87124, USA
Toll-Free Phone: (800) 995-2138
Phone: 505-896-3522
**www.uspca.com**

**Canadian Personal Chef Alliance**
205 Richmond St west
Toronto, Ontario
Canada, M5V-1V3
416-486-6471
877-402-3221
**www.cpcalliance.com**


**Vancouver Personal Chef Network**
**www.vancouverpersonalchef.co**


**Personal Chef  United Kingdom**
**www.personalchef.uk.com**


**Big City Chefs**
Nationwide organization that provides restaurant quality personal chefs that have professional culinary experience.
P.O. Box 232206
San Diego, CA 92193
1-866-321-CHEF
1-866-321-2433
**www.bigcitychefs.com**


# Professional Culinary Associations & Organizations

### International Association of Culinary Professionals
IACP is a not-for-profit professional association that provides continuing education and development for its members who are engaged in the areas of culinary education, communication, or in the preparation of food and drink.  The Worldwide membership of nearly 4,000 encompasses over 35 countries and is literally a "Who's Who" of the world of food. This diversity not only offers unique insight into the world's cuisines, but provides excellent networking opportunities.  IACP's vision

is to be a worldwide forum for the lively development and exchange of information, knowledge, and inspiration within the professional food community.

304 West Liberty Street - Suite 201
Louisville, KY 40202
Telephone US (502) 581-9786
Fax US (502) 589-3602
www.iacp.com


## Personal Chef Directory Listing Service

**Chefhound.com**
Personal Chef locator that is free to all registrants at **personalchefmarketing.com.**

**http://www.pchefnet.com.**
You can obtain a free listing that is international in scope. It currently includes listings from personal chefs across the US and Canada where the personal chef industry is experiencing its most rapid growth.


## Chef's Clothing Web sites

www.chefwear.com
www.ebay.com
www.kingmenus.com
www.culinaryclassics.com
www.chefsemporium.net
www.crookedbrook.com
www.chefswork.com
www.gourmetgear.com
www.chefsuniforms.com
www.kitchenkapers.com
www.thekitchenstore.com
www.125west.com
www.thechefshop.com
www.thecorporatedepot.com
www.foodserviceunlimited.com

## Training

Culinary Business Academy
4150 W. Peoria Ave.
Suite 220
Phoenix, AZ 85029
1-800-747-2433

## Chef Jewelry

This is a great site if you are looking for cooking related jewelry including pins, bracelets, charms, magnets, papergoods, and more. Guys, check it out, too. You might find something for yourself or the women in your life!

**www.thejewelrykitchen.com**

## Web site Hosting

**Ezchef.net**

# Appendix B

# *Food Safety Resources*

## ServSafe® Certification

Created by the industry, for the industry, the ServSafe food safety training program is one of the industry's strongest educational tools administered by the National Restaurant Association Educational Foundation (NRAEF). ServSafe is the recommended food safety training program for the personal chef industry.

**http://www.nraef.org/catalog/**

## Other Food Safety Resources

**Washington State University**
Two web site resources relating to Food Safety for Consumers.

**http://www.foodsafety.wsu.edu/**

**The Penn State Food Safety Web Site**

The Penn State Department of Food Science has recently created a new information resource for extension educators, the food industry, and consumers interested in the safety of our food supply. The Penn State Food Safety Web Site combines a user-friendly environment with a farm-to-fork approach for quick retrieval of food safety information pertaining to the entire food system. Unique to this site are two databases with over 1300 links to online food safety resources.

**http://foodsafety.cas.psu.edu/**

**University of California, at Davis**

This web site provides useful information about food safety issues.

**http://foodsafe.ucdavis.edu/**

**The Food Safety Training and Education Alliance for Retail, Food Service, Vending, Institutions, and Regulators (FSTEA) was born out of the President's Food Safety Initiative of 1997. This site links to state and local food codes.**

http://www.fstea.org/resources/foodcodes.html

**USDA Food borne Illness Education Information Center**

The USDA/FDA Food borne Illness Education Information Center provides information about food borne illness prevention to education, trainers, and organizations. Here you can find the Educational Materials Database, which includes everything from posters, games, computer software, and teaching guides for elementary and secondary schools, as well as training materials for managers and employees of the food industry.

**http://www.nal.usda.gov/fnic/foodborne/wais.shtml**

# Appendix C

# *Marketing Worksheet*

I.  MARKET ANALYSIS
   A. Target Market - Who are the customers?
      1. I will be selling primarily to (check all that apply):

|  | | Total Percent of Business |
|---|---|---|
| a. Busy Families | _____ | _____ |
| b. Wealthy Families | _____ | _____ |
| c. Medical Needs | _____ | _____ |
| d. Health/Diet | _____ | _____ |
| e. Don't Like/Can't Cook | _____ | _____ |
| f. Other | _____ | _____ |

2. I will be targeting customers by:

   a. Types of Service (i.e. Bi-Weekly, Monthly, etc) _____
   b. Geographic area? Which areas?   _____
   c. Sales? We will target sales of  _____
   d. Demographic? My ideal client is _____
   e. Other?   _____

3. How much will my selected market spend on our type
   of product or service this coming year? Estimate.
   $_____

B. Competition
   1. Who are my competitors?

   NAME _____
   ADDRESS _____
   _____

   Years in Business _____
   Market Share          _____
   Price/Strategy        _____
   Product/Service
       Features          _____

   NAME _____
   ADDRESS _____
   _____

   Years in Business _____
   Market Share          _____
   Price/Strategy        _____
   Product/Service
       Features          _____

   2. How competitive is the market?

   High        _____
   Medium      _____
   Low         _____

   3. List below your strengths and weaknesses compared to
      your competition (consider such areas as location, reputation, services, pricing,
      etc.):

   Strengths                    Weaknesses

   1._____    1._____
   2._____    2._____
   3._____    3._____
   4._____    4._____

C. Environment

   1. The following are some important economic factors
      that will affect my product or service (such as
      trade area growth, industry health, economic trends,
      taxes, rising food prices, etc.):

   _____

_____
_____

2. The following are some important legal factors that
   will affect my market:

_____
_____
_____

3. The following are some important government factors:

_____
_____
_____

## II. PRODUCT OR SERVICE ANALYSIS
### A. Description
1. Describe here what the product/service is and what it does:

_____
_____
_____

### B. Comparison
1. What advantages does my service have over
   those of the competition (consider such things as expertise, special training,
   etc.)?

_____
_____
_____

2. What disadvantages does it have?

_____
_____
_____

### C. Some Considerations
1. Where will you get your groceries, cookware, other supplies?

_____
_____
_____

2. List other considerations:

_____
_____

## III. MARKETING STRATEGIES - MARKET MIX

### A. Image

    1. First, what kind of image do I want to have (such as cheap but good, or exclusiveness, or customer-oriented or highest quality, or convenience, or speed, or ...)?

_____

### B. Features & Benefits
    1. The features I will emphasize:

        a. _____

        b. _____

        c. _____

    2. The benefits of each feature is:

### C. Pricing
    1. I will be using the following pricing strategy:

    2. Are my prices in line with our image?
        YES\_\_\_        NO\_\_\_

    3. Do my prices cover costs and leave a margin of profit?
        YES\_\_\_        NO\_\_\_

### D. Customer Services
    1. List the customer services you provide:

a. _____

b. _____

c. _____

2. These are my sales/credit terms:

a. _____

b. _____

c._____

3. The competition offers the following services:

a. _____

b. _____

c._____

E. Advertising/Promotion

1. These are the things I wish to say about my business:

_____

_____

_____

2. We will use the following advertising/promotion sources:

1. Television          _____

2. Radio               _____

3. Direct mail         _____

4. Personal contacts   _____

5. Trade associations  _____

6. Newspaper           _____

7. Magazines           _____

8. Yellow Pages        _____

9. Billboard           _____

10. Other_____       _____

3. The following are the reasons why I consider the media I have chosen to be the most effective:

_____

_____

_____

# Appendix D

# *Marketing & Sales Resources*

## Marketing Books

**The Tipping Point: How Little Things Can Make a Big Differenc**
by Malcolm Gladwell

**Purple Cow: Transform Your Business by Being Remarkable**
by Seth Godin

**Positioning: The Battle for Your Mind**
by Al Ries and Jack Trout

**101 Ways to Promote Yourself: Tricks of the Trade for Taking Charge of Your Own Success**
by Raleigh Pinskey

**Thinking for a Living: Creating Ideas that Revitalize Your Business, Career and Life**
by Joey Reiman

**Your Marketing Sucks!**
by Mark Stevens

**Get Clients Now! A 28-Day Marketing Program for Professionals and Consultants**
by C.J. Hayden

**The Fall of Advertising and The Rise of PR**
by Al and Laura Ries

**Fool-Proof Marketing: 15 Winning Methods for Selling Any Product or Service in Any Economy**
by Robert W. Bly

**Marketing Outrageously**
by Jon Spoelstra and Mark Cuban

**Ice to the Eskimos: How to Market a Product that Nobody Wants**
by Jon Spoelstra

**Getting Business to Come to You: A Complete Do-It-Yourself Guide to Attracting All the Business You Can Enjoy**
by Paul Edwards, Sara Edwards, Laura Clampitt Douglas

**What Clients Love: A Field Guide to Growing Your Business**
by Harry Beckwith

## Sales Books

**How to Master the Art of Selling**
by Tom Hopkins

**Tom Hopkin's Low Profile Selling**
by Tom Hopkins

**The Greatest Salesman In the World**
by Og Mandino

**Selling for Dummies**
by Tom Hopkins

**How to Sell Yourself**
by Joe Girard

# Appendix E

# *Freezing Meals Menu Resources*

Here are a few resources that I recommend when planning your menu:

## Web sites

www.recipesource.com/misc/freezer/indexall.html
http://www.dvo.com/freezermeals.html
http://www.30daygourmet.com/
http://snider.mardox.com/plans.htm

## Books

**Frozen Assets: How to Cook for a Day and Eat for a Month**
by Deborah Taylor-Houg

**Once-a-Month Cooking**
by Mimi Wilson and Mary Beth Langerborg

**Dinner's in the Freezer: More Mary, Less Martha**
by Jill Bond

**The Freezer Cooking Manual**
by Nanci Slagle and Tara Wohlenhaus

**Month of Meals**
by Kelly Machel

**The Southern Living Complete Do-Ahead Cookbook**
by Ann H. Harvey

**Prevention's Freezer Cookbook**
by Sharon Sanders

# Appendix F

# *Favorite Recipes*

Here are some of the recipes that my clients enjoy. Some recipes are ones that I have collected through the year from a variety of sources including family members.

Others were ones that I discovered on what I consider to be the best Internet web site for recipe and cooking information, CooksRecipes.Com. This web site, designed and maintained by Hope Pryor, contains over 12,000 recipes. Many of them are Hope's very own recipes. I encourage you to visit her very informative web site that, besides the recipes, contains a thorough cooking dictionary, cooking tips, cooking forums, and more.

# Beef and Broccoli Stir-Fry

The key to success with any type of stir-fry, is to have the ingredients prepped and ready before the cooking begins.

**8 ounces top sirloin, cut into 1/4-inch-thick strips**
**3 tablespoons soy sauce**
**1 tablespoon Sherry**
**1 tablespoon brown sugar**
**1 tablespoon oriental sesame oil**
**3 large garlic cloves, minced**
**1 2-inch piece fresh ginger, peeled, minced**
**2 cups broccoli florets**
**1 tablespoon peanut or vegetable oil**
**2 cups Chinese pea pods, trimmed**
**6 green onions, cut into 1-inch-long pieces**
**1/2 red bell pepper, sliced**
**1 teaspoon cornstarch**

1)  Combine first 7 ingredients and refrigerate 4 hours or overnight.

2)  Cook broccoli in small pot of boiling salted water until almost crisp-tender, about 2 minutes; drain. Rinse under cold water to cool.

3)  Heat oil in wok or heavy large skillet over high heat. Using slotted spoon, transfer beef to wok, reserving marinade. Stir-fry beef until just browned, about 2 minutes. Remove beef from wok. Add broccoli, pea pods, green onions and red bell pepper. Continue stir-frying until vegetables are just crisp-tender, about 3 minutes.

4)  Stir cornstarch into reserved marinade. Pour marinade over vegetables in wok. Add beef and stir-fry until liquid boils and thickens, about 1 minute.

Serves 2. (Recipe may be doubled.)

# Beef Burgundy

**This hearty French stew makes a wonderful entree for a buffet dinner, since it doesn't require much last-minute attention. A perfect selection for no-fuss entertaining. Bouquet garni (directions at bottom of recipe)**

**1/4 cup butter or margarine**
**16 small white boiling onions, peeled**
**6 slices bacon, diced**
**4 pounds boneless beef chuck, trimmed of fat and cut into 1 1/2-inch cubes**
**1/4 cup brandy, warmed (optional)**
**2 cups burgundy or other dry red wine**
**2 garlic cloves, peeled**
**2 cups small mushrooms, sliced**
**1 1/2 cups water**
**6 tablespoons all-purpose flour**
**1/2 cup cold water**
**Salt and pepper**
**Hot cooked rice or noodles (optional)**

1) Prepare bouquet garni; set side.

2) Melt butter in a large, heavy pan over medium heat. Add onions and bacon; cook, stirring often, until onions are lightly browned, about 10 minutes. lift out onions and bacon with a slotted spoon and set aside.

3) Add beef to pan, a portion at a time (do not crowd pan). Cook, turning as needed, until well browned on all sides. If using brandy, move pan into an open area, away from exhaust fans and flammable items. Add brandy to pan and ignite; shake or tilt pan until flame dies.

4) Return all meat to pan; add burgundy, garlic, mushrooms, the 1 1/2 cups water, bouquet garni, onions, and bacon. Bring to a boil; then reduce heat, cover, and simmer until meat is tender when pierced, about 1 1/2 hours. With a slotted spoon, transfer meat, mushrooms, and onions to a serving dish; keep warm.

5) Pour meat juices through a fine wire strainer set over a medium-size pan; discard residue in strainer.

6) In a small bowl, mix flour and the 1/2 cup water to make a smooth paste. Stir flour mixture into meat juices; cook over medium heat, stirring constantly, until sauce is thick and smooth. Season to taste with salt and pepper.

7) Pour sauce over meat and vegetables. If made ahead, let cool; then cover and refrigerate until next day. To reheat, transfer to a baking dish; cover and bake in a 350*F (175*C) oven until bubbly and heated through, about 35 minutes.

8) Serve over hot cooked rice or noodles, if desired.

Makes 8 servings.

**Bouquet garni:** Tie in a square of damp cheesecloth: 1 carrot (quartered), 1 celery top, 1 dry bay leaf, 1 or 2 parsley sprigs, and 1 fresh thyme sprig (or 1 teaspoon dry thyme).

# Beef Stroganoff with Noodles

For this make-ahead classic, the beef mixture can easily be prepared in advance and refrigerated (or frozen). To serve, cook the noodles while you reheat the meat and sauce; stir sour cream into the sauce at the very last.

**2 pounds round steak, cut 1-inch thick**
**3 tablespoons vegetable or olive oil**
**1/4 cup dry red wine**
**1/2 pound small white boiling onions, peeled**
**1/2 pound mushrooms, sliced**
**1 garlic clove, minced or pressed**
**3 tablespoons all-purpose flour**
**1 (10 1/2-ounce) can condensed consomme**
**1/4 cup tomato paste**
**Salt and pepper**
**1 dry bay leaf**
**8 ounces dry medium-wide noodles**
**1/2 cup sour cream**
**2 tablespoons chopped parsley**

1) Cut steak across the grain into 1/4-inch thick slices.

2) Heat 1 1/2 tablespoons of the oil in a wide frying pan over medium-high heat. Add meat, a portion at a time (do not crowd pan); cook, turning as needed, until browned on all sides. Transfer to a 3-quart baking dish. Stir in wine.

3) Heat remaining 1 1/2 tablespoons oil in pan. Add onions and cook over medium heat, stirring often, until golden, about 7 minutes.

4) Add mushrooms and garlic; cook, stirring often, until mushrooms are limp. With a slotted spoon, transfer vegetables to baking dish.

5) Stir flour into drippings in pan; cook, stirring, until flour is golden. Remove from heat and gradually stir in consomme and tomato paste. Season to taste with salt and pepper. Return to high heat and bring sauce to a boil, stirring; pour sauce over meat and vegetables. Add bay leaf, cover, and bake in a 350*F (175*C) oven until meat is tender to bite, about 1 1/2 hours. if made ahead, let cool; then cover and refrigerate until next day (freeze for longer storage). Reheat before serving.

6) To serve, in a large pan, cook noodles in about 2 1/2 quarts of boiling salted water until al dente (firm to the bite), about 6 to 8 minutes; or cook according to package directions.

7)    Drain noodles and spoon into center of a rimmed serving dish. Stir sour cream into hot meat mixture. Spoon meat mixture over noodles and sprinkle with parsley.

Makes 6 servings.

# Sirloin Kebabs with Fresh Pineapple

**1/4 cup lemon-lime carbonated beverage**
**1/4 cup dry sherry**
**1/4 cup soy sauce**
**3 tablespoons sugar**
**3 tablespoons white vinegar**
**1/2 teaspoons garlic powder**
**1/4 teaspoon salt**
**1/4 teaspoon freshly ground pepper**
**2 pounds sirloin steak, cut into 1-inch cubes**
**2 medium onions, cut into wedges**
**1/2 pound fresh whole mushrooms**
**2 medium green, red or yellow bell peppers (or combination)**
**1 small pineapple, cut into 1-inch chunks**
**Wooden skewers, soaked in water for 30 minutes**

1) Combine first 8 ingredients in a large shallow, nonreactive dish. Add beef cubes; cover and marinate for 1 hour at room temperature or a minimum of 2 hours to overnight in the refrigerator. Remove beef cubes from marinade, reserving marinade.

2) Alternately thread beef cubes, onion, mushrooms, green pepper and pineapple onto prepared skewers.

3) Grill, covered, over medium-hot coals (350* to 400*F / 175* to 205*C) 10 to 12 minutes or until desired doneness, turning and basting occasionally with reserved marinade. Discard any remaining marinade.

Serves 4 to 6.

# Irish Beef Stew

**2 pounds lean beef stew or chuck, in two inch chunks**
**1 teaspoon salt**
**1/2 teaspoon pepper**
**Flour for dredging**
**2 tablespoons bacon drippings or vegetable oil**
**2 large yellow onions, chopped**
**1 garlic clove, finely minced (optional)**
**6 to 8 medium carrots, scraped and sliced**
**2 to 3 large potatoes, peeled and cut into cubes**
**2 to 3 turnips, peeled and cut into cubes (optional)**
**1 cup Guiness stout**
**1 cup beef broth**

1) Season beef with salt and pepper; toss beef chunks in flour until well coated.

2) Heat drippings or oil in Dutch oven and brown beef over medium-high heat in two batches. When all are browned, remove beef from pan and add onions and garlic and cook over medium heat until onion is translucent.

3) Return beef to pot and add carrots, potatoes, turnips, stout and broth. Bring to a boil and reduce heat to a simmer. Cover and cook for 2 hours or until beef is fork-tender.

Makes 6 to 8 servings.

# Sirloin Tips with Mushrooms

**11/2 pounds sirloin tips, cubed**
**2 tablespoons butter**
**1 tablespoon vegetable oil**
**1/2 pound fresh mushrooms, sliced**
**2 garlic cloves, finely minced**
**2 teaspoons Dijon-style mustard**
**2 teaspoons cornstarch**
**2/3 cup heavy cream**
**2/3 cup beef broth**
**1/4 cup white wine vinegar**
**1 tablespoon soy sauce**
**2 teaspoons dried parsley**
**Hot cooked, buttered noodles**

1) In a large skillet, brown meat in butter and oil; transfer to a 2-quart baking dish.

2) In the same skillet, saute mushrooms and garlic until mushrooms are tender, about 3 minutes. Pour mushrooms and liquid over meat. Cover and bake at 300*F (150*C) for 2 hours or until meat is tender.

3) In small bowl, combine mustard, cornstarch and cream; set aside.

4) In skillet, combine broth, vinegar, soy sauce and parsley; bring to a boil. Boil for 2 minutes; stir in mustard/cream mixture, bring to a boil and cook 2 minutes, stirring constantly. Drain juices from the baking dish into broth mixture. Cook over medium heat, stirring constantly until thickened and bubbly. Add beef mixture and combine well.

5) Serve over hot buttered noodles.

Makes 4 to 6 servings.

# Fancy Yankee Pot Roast

**1/4 cup pure olive oil**
**3 onions, sliced**
**One 3 to 4-pound top or bottom round beef roast**
**Flour for dredging**
**8 slender carrots, or fatter ones cut in half or quartered**
**3 ribs celery, cut in half**
**2 1/2 cups beef broth**
**1 1/2 cups hearty red wine**
**5 to 6 sprigs fresh thyme**
**1 rounded teaspoon freshly ground black pepper**
**Salt to taste**
**2 tablespoons unsalted butter, at room temperature**
**2 rounded tablespoons flour**

1) In a large, heavy flameproof casserole, preferably cast iron, over medium heat, heat the olive oil and sauté the onions until golden. Thoroughly dredge the beef in the flour, covering all the surfaces. Add to the pan and brown on all sides. The flour may cause the onions to burn slightly. This is good and will add lots of flavor. Add the carrots, celery, beef broth, wine, thyme, black pepper and salt to taste. Reduce heat, partially cover, and barely simmer for 3 to 3 1/2 hours, turning the beef occasionally. Remove the carrots and celery when they are cooked and reserve.

2) When the beef is falling apart tender, remove it from the broth. Remove the thyme sprigs. Knead the butter and 2 tablespoons flour together until thoroughly combined. Add the mixture to the broth and stir with a wooden spoon until you have a sauce the consistency of buttermilk. Remove from the heat.

3) To serve, slice the beef and arrange on a platter. Cover with some of the sauce. Put the remaining sauce in a bowl or gravy boat. Arrange the carrots and celery attractively on the beef platter. Garnish with fresh thyme sprigs, if you like. Serve immediately.

## Serves 6

# Cajun-Style Rib-Eye Steak

**Begin marinating the steaks a day ahead.**

**1 cup vegetable oil**
**1 onion, thinly sliced**
**1 tablespoon garlic powder**
**1 tablespoon plus 1/2 teaspoon black pepper**
**6 small rib-eye steaks, approximately 3 pounds**
**1 tablespoon paprika**
**1 teaspoon cayenne pepper, or to taste**
**1 teaspoon salt**
**1/2 teaspoon white pepper**

1) Combine oil, sliced onion, garlic powder and 1 tablespoon black pepper in 13 x 9 x 2-inch glass baking dish. Add steaks to marinade, turning to coat. Spoon half of sliced onion evenly over steaks. Cover and refrigerate overnight.

2) Prepare barbecue (medium-high heat) or preheat broiler. Remove steaks from marinade. Combine paprika, cayenne, salt, white pepper and 1/2 teaspoon black pepper in small bowl. Sprinkle each side of each steak with 1 teaspoon spice mixture.

3) Grill or broil steaks until cooked through, about 8 minutes per side for medium-rare. Cut each steak in half. Divide steaks among plates; serve.

**Serves 6**

# Savory Swiss Steak

Lean round steak, tenderized by pounding with a meat mallet, gains lusty flavor from a hearty tomato-vegetable sauce in this recipe. you can simmer the meat on the range or, if you prefer, bake it in the oven.

**1/2 cup all-purpose flour**
**1 tablespoon dry mustard**
**1 1/2 pounds round steak, cut 1-inch thick**
**2 tablespoons vegetable oil or bacon drippings**
**1 (14 1/2-ounce) can diced tomatoes**
**1 cup sliced onions**
**1/2 cup diced celery**
**2 or 3 carrots, diced**
**2 tablespoons Worcestershire sauce**
**1 tablespoon brown sugar, firmly packed**
**Salt and pepper**

1) Mix flour with mustard. Sprinkle flour mixture over steak and pound it in with a cleated meat mallet. Cut pounded steak into serving-size pieces.

2) Heat oil in a wide, heavy frying pan over medium-high heat. add meat and cook, turning once, until browned on both sides. If you a baking meat, transfer it to a shallow baking pan.

3) Add tomatoes and their liquid, onions, celery, carrots, Worcestershire and sugar to meat in baking pan or frying pan. Season to taste with salt and pepper.

4) Cover and bake in a 350*F (175*C) oven (or bring to a boil, then reduce heat, cover and simmer) until meat is tender when pierced, about 1 1/2 hours.

Makes 4 servings.

# Salisbury Steak

**1 pound ground chuck**
**1/2 teaspoon taco seasoning**
**4 green onions**
**1/2 cup shredded cheddar cheese**
**1(10 3/4-ounce) can condensed mushroom soup**
**Salt and pepper to taste**

1) Press the ground chuck into two 1/2-pound patties, then sprinkle with taco seasoning, salt and pepper.

2) Grill or fry until brown then place in a baking dish (editor's note: stove-top safe) and cover with diced green onions and shredded cheese.

3) Mix soup with about a half can of water and pour mixture over patties; let simmer, covered, on low heat at least 20 minutes or until ready to serve. Very good.

# Polenta Lasagna with Spinach

**1 tablespoon olive oil**
**1 small onion, very finely chopped**
**1 garlic clove, minced**
**1/2 teaspoon salt**
**7 cups chicken stock**
**2 cups instant polenta (one 13.2 ounce box)**
**7 tablespoons freshly grated Parmesan cheese**
**2 packages (10 ounces each) frozen, chopped spinach, thawed**
**2 containers (15 ounces each) low-fat ricotta cheese**
**Salt and freshly ground pepper**
**Pinch of nutmeg**
**Prepared Tomato Sauce, about 3 to 4 cups (recipe follows)**
**2 cups shredded mozzarella cheese**

1) Lightly spray a 13 x 9 x 2-inch baking dish with non-stick cooking spray. In a large saucepan, warm the olive oil over medium heat. Add the onion and sauté for 3 to 5 minutes or until softened. Add the garlic and sauté 1 minute more, making sure it doesn't brown. Add salt and stock and bring to a rolling boil over medium heat.

2) In a thin stream very slowly add the polenta stirring constantly with a wooden spoon. Reduce the heat to low and continue cooking for 3 to 5 minutes, stirring constantly to be sure it doesn't stick, until it's thick and creamy. Stir in 3 tablespoons of the Parmesan cheese.

3) Pour polenta into the prepared baking dish, smoothing the top with a rubber spatula if necessary. Let polenta rest for at least 2 hours. (Can be made up to 3 days ahead however.)

4) Squeeze out all the water from the spinach. In a small bowl mix spinach with ricotta. Season with salt, pepper and nutmeg.

5) Preheat oven to 375*F (190*C).

6) Invert the polenta onto a cutting surface. Set the dish aside to use again. Cut the polenta rectangle in half to make 2 rectangles each measuring 9 x 6 1/2- inches. Slice each rectangle lengthwise in half again, using a long piece of dental floss or a serrated knife to make the job easiest, creating 4 layers (each 9 x 6 1/2-inches).

7) Spoon prepared tomato sauce evenly on the bottom of the 13 x 9 x 2-inch baking dish. Place two of the polenta pieces in the dish to cover the bottom. Spoon half of the spinach ricotta mixture over the polenta, using the back of a spoon to spread it out, and then sprinkle with 1 cup mozzarella and 2 tablespoons Parmesan. Spoon 2 cups of sauce over cheese.

8) Top with remaining polenta pieces and finish with a layer of cheese.

9) Place the lasagna dish on a baking sheet to catch any drips. Bake uncovered for 30 minutes. Remove from the oven and let sit for 10 minutes.

## Serves 6 to 8

### Tomato Sauce

2 tablespoons olive or vegetable oil
1 large onion, chopped
1 (15-ounce) can tomato sauce
1 (6-ounce) can tomato paste
1/2 cup dry red wine
1 teaspoon dry oregano leaves
1 teaspoon dry basil leaves
Salt to taste

1) Heat oil in a wide frying pan over medium heat; add onion and cook, stirring often, until softened, about 5 minutes.

2) Stir in tomato sauce, tomato paste, wine, oregano and basil. Bring to a simmer; then simmer, uncovered, for 10 minutes. Season to taste with salt.

Makes about 4 cups sauce.

# Lip Lickin' Lasagna

**2 pounds hamburger meat**
**1 medium onion, chopped**
**2 (15-ounce) cans tomato sauce**
**1 teaspoon Italian seasoning**
**1 box lasagna noodles**
**2 (8-ounce) packages mozzarella cheese**
**1 (8-ounce) package cheddar cheese**
**1 (8-ounce) package Parmesan cheese**
**1 cup cottage cheese**

1) Brown hamburger and onion in skillet. Drain out excess juices. Add tomato sauce and Italian seasoning. Simmer on low heat.

2) Cook noodles according to directions on box.

3) On bottom layer of lasagna, spread half of meat mixture. Next, add cottage cheese. Sprinkle one bag of mozzarella, one half bag of cheddar and one half bag Parmesan. Add layer of noodles. Repeat meat and cheese, leaving about a handful of mozzarella, cheddar, and Parmesan cheeses out for topping. Add one more very thin layer of noodles. Sprinkle cheeses for topping. Bake at 400*F (205*C) until cheese is melted and top is starting to brown. Takes approximately 45 minutes depending on oven. Cut into 12 squares and serve.

Makes: Up to 12 servings

# Portobella Lasagna

**8 ounces lasagna noodles (9 noodles)**
**2 (6-ounce) packages sliced Portobellas**
**1/2 teaspoon salt**
**1/4 cup water**
**1/4 teaspoon fennel seed (or anise seed)**
**1/4 teaspoon dried basil leaves, crushed**
**1/4 teaspoon dried oregano leaves, crushed**
**1 (28-ounce) jar marinara or spaghetti sauce**
**1 (15-ounce) container ricotta cheese**
**1 egg**
**Salt and freshly ground pepper**
**1/2 cup freshly grated Parmesan cheese, divided**
**3 cups (12 ounces) shredded mozzarella**

1) Preheat the oven to 350*F (175*C). Follow package directions and cook lasagna noodles al dente.

2) Place the mushrooms in a Dutch oven, add salt and water. Cover and bring to a boil over high heat; remove the lid, add fennel, basil and oregano, stir, and cover again. Reduce heat to medium-low. Cook for 6 to 8 minutes. The mushrooms will have released much of their liquid and there should be about 1/2 cup in the pot.

3) With slotted spoon, remove mushrooms out of the liquid and set aside. Over high heat, reduce the remaining liquid to 2 to 3 tablespoons. Add the marinara sauce; mixing well. Remove from heat.

4) In small bowl, combine ricotta, egg and 1/4 cup Parmesan cheese; season with salt and pepper; mix well.

5) To assemble the lasagna, layer 3 noodles in the bottom of a lightly greased 13 x 9 x 2 - inch baking dish. In the order given, spread 1/3 of the ricotta mixture, 1/2 cup of mozzarella 1/3 of the mushrooms and 1/3 of the sauce. Repeat two more times. For the top layer, sprinkle the remaining Parmesan and mozzarella cheese on top. Cover the pan with aluminum foil, and bake for 20 minutes, or until heated thorough. Remove cover last 5 minutes of baking. Allow lasagna to sit for 15 minutes to before serving.

## Serves 6 to 8

# Spinach Veggie Rice Casserole

**1 1/2 cups cooked brown rice**
**1 cup chopped fine spinach**
**1 1/3 cups chopped water chestnuts**
**1/2 cup celery**
**1/2 cup red pepper**
**1/3 cup chicken-flavored gravy**
**2/3 cup bread crumbs, buttered**

1) Mix together rice, spinach, chestnuts, celery, gravy and pepper and turn into a lightly greased casserole dish.

2) Sprinkle top with buttered bread crumbs and bake for 30 minutes at 350*F (175*C).

## Makes 4 servings

# Angel Hair Pasta with Lemon and Garlic

This makes a light, satisfying main course, ideal for a hot summer evening supper.

**1 pound angel hair pasta**
**1/2 cup fresh basil, chopped**
**1/2 cup fresh Parmesan cheese, grated**
**2 tablespoons olive oil**
**6 to 8 cloves garlic, minced**
**1 1/4 cups dry white wine**
**1/2 cup fresh lemon juice**
**2 1/2 cups chopped ripe tomato**
**1 teaspoon salt**
**Freshly ground black pepper to taste**
**Parmesan cheese, freshly grated**

1) Measure and prepare all ingredients in advance.

2) Cook the pasta and place in large serving bowl. Add the basil and Parmesan cheese; set aside *and keep warm.*

3) In large a skillet heat the olive oil and saute the garlic just until it begins to change color. Remove skillet from heat and add the wine. Return to the heat and cook for another 2 to 3 minutes, or until the wine has been reduced by half. Stir in the lemon juice and tomato and remove from heat.

4) Pour hot lemon/tomato mixture over pasta mixture in the serving bowl, add salt and pepper to taste. Toss to mix.

5) Serve garnished with Parmesan cheese.

Serves 4

# Baked Spaghetti Florentine

This versatile dish can be served as a main or side dish, and it's a great way to get the kids to eat their spinach!

**1 egg, beaten**
**2 teaspoons minced dried onion**
**1/2 cup sour cream**
**1/4 cup milk**
**1/2 teaspoon salt**
**Freshly ground pepper to taste**
**2 cups (16-ounces) shredded Monterey Jack cheese**
**1(10-ounce) package frozen spinach, thawed and squeezed dry**
**4 ounces spaghetti, cooked and drained**
**4 tablespoons freshly grated Parmesan cheese**

1) Preheat oven to 350*F (175*C). Lightly grease a 10 x 6 x 2-inch baking dish. Set aside.

2) In a large bowl, combine egg, onion, sour cream, milk, salt, pepper, and 2 tablespoons Parmesan cheese. Add Monterey Jack cheese; mix well.

3) Add the spinach and cooked spaghetti and toss to combine well. Place mixture in the prepared baking dish and sprinkle with remaining Parmesan.

4) Bake for 15 minutes covered; remove cover and continue baking for additional 15 minutes.

Makes 2 to 4 servings

# Baked Ziti with Three Cheeses

**2 tablespoons olive oil**
**1 onion, chopped**
**4 garlic cloves, finely minced**
**1 teaspoon fennel seeds**
**1 teaspoon dried oregano, crumbled**
**1/2 teaspoon dried rubbed sage**
**1 (6-ounce) can tomato paste**
**1 (14-ounce) can Italian-style stewed tomatoes**
**1 cup water**
**1/2 cup freshly grated Parmesan cheese, divided**
**Salt and freshly ground black pepper to taste**
**1 (15-ounce) container ricotta cheese**
**1 egg**
**2 cups grated mozzarella cheese**
**12 ounces rigatoni pasta, cooked according to p ackage directions**

1) Heat oil in large saucepan over medium-low heat. Add onion, garlic and fennel seeds and sauté until onion has softened, about 5 minutes. Stir in oregano and sage, cook 30 seconds and add tomato paste and cook for 1 minute. Add tomatoes and water. Simmer until mixture thickens slightly, stirring occasionally, about 10 minutes. Stir in 1/4 cup Parmesan. Season with salt and pepper.

2) Preheat oven to 425*F (220*C). Grease a 9 x 13 x 2-inch glass baking dish.

3) In medium bowl combine ricotta cheese and egg. Season with salt and pepper.

4) Spread 1/4 of sauce over bottom of prepared baking dish. Layer 1/3 of cooked pasta over. Drop half of ricotta mixture over by spoonfuls and sprinkle with 1/3 of the mozzarella then ladle 1/4 of sauce over . Repeat layering with another 1/3 of pasta, remaining ricotta mixture, 1/3 of the mozzarella, 1/4 of sauce and remaining pasta. Ladle remaining sauce over and sprinkle with remaining 1/3 of mozzarella and remaining 1/4 cup Parmesan.

5) Cover casserole with aluminum foil and bake until heated through, about 45 minutes, removing cover after 30 minutes to allow cheese to brown.

Serves 6

# Fettuccine Alfredo

Italian restaurateur Alfredo di Lello is credited with creating this dish in the 1920s. The fettuccine is enrobed in a rich, yet simple sauce of butter, grated Parmesan cheese, heavy cream and freshly ground black pepper...and nothing more.

**1 (16-ounce) package fettuccine pasta**
**1/2 cup butter**
**2 cups heavy cream**
**1 cup freshly grated Parmigiano Reggiano (see note)**
**1 teaspoon salt**
**Freshly ground black pepper to taste**
**Freshly grated Parmesan cheese as accompaniment**

1)    Cook pasta according to package directions.

2)    While pasta is being prepared, melt butter in large skillet; add cream, salt and pepper. Bring to a boil and simmer for a few minutes uncovered to to reduce and thicken sauce. Remove from heat and add cooked fettuccini and 1 cup Parmesan. Toss to combine and serve immediately with an extra sprinkling of Parmesan cheese over the top, if desired.

**Serves 4**

# Pasta with Tomatoes, Zucchini and Pesto

This delicious pasta dish makes use of convenient ready-made pesto, available in your grocer's refrigerated section.

**1/4 cup olive oil**
**4 cups 1/2-inch cubes zucchini**
**1 1/2 cups chopped onion**
**2 large garlic cloves, chopped**
**1 (28-ounce) can diced tomatoes in juice**
**1 pound spaghetti**
**1 (7-ounce) package purchased pesto**
**1/2 cup packed, thinly sliced fresh basil**
**Salt and freshly ground pepper to taste**
**Freshly grated Parmesan cheese**

1) Heat oil in heavy large pot over medium-high heat. Add zucchini, onion and garlic and sauté until zucchini is crisp-tender, about 5 minutes. Add tomatoes with juices and simmer until almost all liquid evaporates, about 8 minutes.

2) Meanwhile, cook pasta in large pot of boiling salted water until just tender but still firm to bite (al dente). Drain but do not rinse; return to pot.

3) Add pesto to pasta and toss to coat. Add zucchini mixture and toss over low heat to combine. Mix in basil. Season pasta with salt and pepper. Transfer pasta to large bowl. Serve, passing Parmesan cheese separately.

Serves 6

# Baked Ham with Pineapple-Seeded Mustard Glaze

**1 (8-pound) bone-in smoked ham (preferably the shank end)**
**1 cup pineapple preserves**
**2 tablespoons Dijon mustard**
**1 1/2 teaspoons yellow mustard seeds**

1) Preheat to 350*F (175*C). Line a roasting pan with aluminum foil.

2) Using a sharp knife, trim off all the skin except for a 1- to 2-inch band around the shank. Trim off all of the fat, leaving a less than 1/4-inch thick layer.

3) In a small bowl, whisk the preserves, Dijon mustard, and mustard seeds, and set aside.

4) Place the ham on a roasting rack in the pan and bake until a meat thermometer inserted in the thickest part of the ham (without touching the bone) registers 140*F (60*C), about 2 hours (allow 15 minutes per pound). After 1 hour, baste with half of the glaze. After 30 minutes, baste with the remaining glaze.

5) Transfer the ham to a carving bowl or platter. Let stand for 15 to 30 minutes before carving.

## Makes 16 to 24 servings

# Cashew Pork and Broccoli

**12 ounces lean boneless pork**
**2 tablespoons soy sauce**
**2 teaspoons toasted sesame oil**
**2 teaspoons finely minced fresh ginger**
**2 garlic cloves, finely minced**
**1/2 cup hoisin sauce**
**1/2 cup water**
**2 tablespoons soy sauce**
**1 tablespoon cornstarch**
**1 teaspoon sugar**
**1/8 teaspoon crushed red pepper**
**1 tablespoon vegetable oil**
**2 medium onions, cut into thin wedges**
**2 celery stalks, thinly bias-sliced**
**3 cups broccoli flowerets**
**Hot cooked rice**
**1/2 cup dry roasted cashews**

1) Trim fat from meat. Thinly slice across the grain into bite-size strips.

2) In a medium bowl, combine meat, 2 tablespoons soy sauce, sesame oil, ginger and garlic. Cover and chill for 1 to 2 hours.

3) For sauce, in a small bowl, stir together hoisin sauce, water, 2 tablespoons soy sauce, cornstarch, sugar and crushed red pepper. Set aside.

4) Add oil to a wok or large skillet. Preheat over medium-high heat (add more oil if necessary during cooking.) Stir-fry onions and celery in hot oil for 1 minute. Add broccoli; stir-fry for 3 to 4 minutes or until crisp-tender. Remove vegetables from wok.

5) Add meat mixture to wok. Stir-fry for 2 to 4 minutes or until desired doneness. Push meat from center of wok.

6) Stir sauce; add to center of wok. Cook and stir until thickened and bubbly. Return cooked vegetables to wok. Stir all ingredients together to coat. Cover and cook about 1 minute more or until heated through.

7) Serve immediately with hot cooked rice. Sprinkle cashews on individual servings.

Makes 4 servings

# Glazed Ham Steak

**1/3 cup spicy brown mustard**
**1/4 cup honey**
**1 teaspoon grated orange peel**
**1 (2-pound) fully cooked ham steak**

1) In a small bowl, combine mustard, honey and orange peel. Brush over one side of ham.

2) Broil or grill, uncovered, over medium-hot heat for 7 minutes. Turn; brush with mustard mixture. Cook until well glazed and heated through, about 7 minutes.

Serves 6

# Apple-Mustard Glazed Ham

The sweet and tangy glaze turns an ordinary baked ham into

a special feast!

**1 cup apple jelly**
**1 tablespoon prepared mustard**
**1 tablespoon lemon juice**
**1/4 teaspoon ground nutmeg**
**1 (5 to 7-pound) fully cooked bone-in ham**
**Whole cloves**

1) In a small saucepan, combine jelly mustard, lemon juice and nutmeg; bring to a boil; stirring constantly. Remove from heat; set aside.

2) Score the surface of the ham, making diamond shapes 1/2-inch deep; insert a clove in each diamond.

3) Place ham on a rack in a shallow roasting pan. Bake, uncover at 325*F (160*C) for 20 minutes per pound or until a meat thermometer reads 140*F (60*C). During the last 30 minutes of baking, brush with glaze twice.

4) Allow ham to sit for 10 minutes before slicing.

Serves 8 to 10

# Apple-Glazed Pork Chops

**1/2 cup teriyaki sauce**
**1 tablespoon lemon juice**
**6 (1/2-inch thick) center-cut pork chops**
**2 cups applesauce**
**2 tablespoons orange marmalade**

1) Combine teriyaki sauce and lemon juice in a 13 x 9 x 2-inch glass baking dish. Arrange pork chops in dish, turning to coat. Cover and marinate 8 hours or overnight in refrigerator, turning meat once.

2) Remove from refrigerator; let stand 30 minutes.

3) Bake, covered at 350*F (175*C) for 45 minutes. Drain all but 2 to 3 tablespoons drippings from dish.

4) Combine applesauce and marmalade; add to baking dish, mixing well with dripping and spooning over pork chops.

5) Return to oven and bake, uncovered, an additional 15 minutes or until done pork chops test done.

## Makes 6 servings

# Pork Chops with Apple Stuffing

**1 (12-ounce) package frozen escalloped apples**

**1/2 stick (1/4 cup) butter or margarine**
**1 small onion, chopped**
**1 celery rib, chopped**
**1 (8-ounce) package herb-seasoned stuffing mix**
**2 tablespoons raisins**
**3/4 cup hot water**
**1 teaspoon chicken bouillon granules**
**6 (1-inch-thick) center-cut pork chops**
**1/4 teaspoon pepper**

1)  Thaw escalloped apples in microwave at MEDIUM (50% power) 6 to 7 minutes. Set aside.

2)  Melt butter in a large skillet over medium heat; add onion and celery, and sauté until tender. Remove from heat.

3)  Stir in stuffing mix, apples, and raisins. Spoon into a lightly greased 13 x 9 x 2-inch baking dish.

4)  Stir together 3/4 cup water and bouillon granules, and pour evenly over stuffing mixture. Arrange pork chops on top, and sprinkle with pepper.

5)  Bake, covered, at 350*F (175*C) for 40 minutes. Uncover and bake 15 more minutes or until done.

## Makes 6 servings

# Sauteed Pork Medallions with Apple and Pear

**4 (3-ounce) pork medallions**
**All-purpose flour for dredging**
**Salt and pepper to taste**
**2 tablespoons butter**
**2 tablespoons finely minced onion**
**1/4 cup apple, pear or plain brandy**
**1 unpeeled apple, cored and finely chopped**
**1 unpeeled pear, cored and finely chopped**
**1/4 cup heavy cream**
**4 ounces cream cheese**

1) Dredge the medallions in flour and season with salt and pepper to taste. Saute the medallions in the butter for approximately 2 to 3 minutes per side. Remove from the skillet and set in a warm place.

2) Add the onion to the skillet and caramelize slightly. Flambe with the brandy.

3) Add the apple, pear and heavy cream. Bring to a boil. Stir in the cream cheese and heat thoroughly; do not boil.

4) Arrange the medallions on a plate and spoon the sauce over top.

## Makes 4 servings

# Chicken Paprika

A classic Hungarian dish, serve with spatzl, egg noodles, or

rice.

**1/4 cup all-purpose flour**
**1 teaspoon salt**
**1 (3 to 3 1/2-pound) chicken, cut into serving pieces**
**2 tablespoons unsalted butter**
**2 tablespoons vegetable oil**
**1 cup chopped yellow onion**
**1/2 cup chopped green bell pepper**
**1 tablespoon paprika (preferably Hungarian)**
**Freshly ground pepper, to taste**
**1 1/2 cups rich chicken stock or canned low-sodium chicken broth**
**1 cup sour cream (do not use nonfat sour cream)**

1) Preheat oven to 350*F (175*C). On a sheet of wax paper, combine flour and salt. Toss chicken pieces in mixture to coat and reserve the excess flour.

2) In a Dutch oven over medium heat, melt butter with oil. Brown chicken, 5 to 10 minutes on each side. Remove to a plate.

3) Reduce temperature to medium. Add onions and bell pepper and sauté until tender, about 5 minutes. Add paprika, pepper, and remaining flour and stir until bubbly. Add stock and stir until thickened.

4) Return chicken to Dutch oven; cover and bake until chicken is no longer pink in the center, about 50 minutes. Blend in sour cream and bake, uncovered, 10 minutes longer.

**Serves 4**

# Crispy Parmesan Chicken

**1 cup fine, dry breadcrumbs**

**1/2 cup grated Parmesan cheese**
**1/4 cup chopped fresh parsley**
**1 teaspoon salt**
**1/4 teaspoon pepper**
**1/2 teaspoon paprika**
**1 stick (1/2 cup) butter or margarine**
**2 garlic cloves, chopped**
**1 (3 to 31/2-pound) package chicken pieces**

1) Stir together first 6 ingredients, and set aside.

2) Place butter and garlic in a shallow microwave-safe dish; microwave at HIGH 1 minute or until butter melts.

3) Dip chicken into garlic butter, and coat evenly with breadcrumb mixture. Arrange chicken on a wire rack in a 15 x 10 x 1-inch jellyroll pan.

4) Bake at 375*F (190*C) for 50 minutes or until chicken is done. Serve immediately.

Makes 4 servings

# Easy Baked Hawaiian Chicken

**1 (20-ounce) can crushed pineapple, undrained**

**1 tablespoon curry powder**
**1 teaspoon sugar**
**3 tablespoons vegetable oil**
**6 to 8 boneless, skinless chicken breast halves**
**1/2 cup flaked coconut**

1) Heat oven to 425*F (220*C) degrees.

2) Pour pineapple with juice into a 13 x 9 x 2-inch baking dish. In a small bowl combine curry powder, sugar and oil.

3) Brush curry mixture on both sides of chicken. Place chicken on top of pineapple, sprinkle with coconut. Bake, uncovered for 30 minutes or until chicken tests done.

Variation: Replace the chicken breasts with ham steak.

# Easy Chicken Pot Pie

**1 refrigerated pie crust (or make your own)**

**3 tablespoons all purpose flour**
**1/4 teaspoon garlic powder**
**1 pound skinless boneless chicken breast, cut into 1-inch pieces**
**3 tablespoons butter**
**2 2/3 cups chicken broth**
**3 cups frozen mixed vegetables**
**1 teaspoon dried rubbed sage**
**Salt and freshly ground black pepper to taste**

1) Preheat oven to 425*F (220*C).

2) Combine flour and garlic powder in medium bowl.

3) Season chicken with salt and pepper. Add chicken to flour; toss to coat.

4) Melt butter in large skillet oven medium-high heat. Add the chicken and any remaining flour to skillet and stir until chicken is brown, about 5 minutes.

5) Stir in broth, vegetables and sage. Bring to boil, scraping up any browned bits. Reduce heat, cover skillet and simmer until chicken is cooked through, about 8 minutes.

6) Season with salt and pepper. Transfer chicken mixture to deep dish 10-inch pie plate or round casserole.

7) op with pie crust; seal and crimp edge and make slits to vent. Bake in oven until crust is golden, about 15 minutes.

## Serves 4 to 6

# Cashew Chicken

**2 teaspoons instant chicken bouillon or base**

**1 1/4 cups boiling water**
**2 tablespoons soy sauce**
**1 tablespoon cornstarch**
**2 teaspoons brown sugar**
**1/2 teaspoon ground ginger**
**1 1/2 pounds boneless, skinless chicken breasts, cut into 1-inch strips**
**2 tablespoons vegetable oil**
**8 ounces sliced fresh mushrooms**
**1/2 cup sliced green onions**
**1 small green pepper, seeded and sliced**
**1 (8-ounce) can sliced water chestnuts, drained**
**1/2 cup cashews**
**Hot cooked rice**

1) Dissolve bouillon or base in water. Set aside.

2) Combine soy sauce, cornstarch, sugar and ginger; set aside.

3) In a large skillet or wok, heat oil over moderately high heat until hot, but not smoking. Stir-fry chicken in vegetable oil until browned. Add onions, green pepper, mushrooms and stir-fry for 2 minutes or until vegetables are crisp-tender. Add water chestnuts and broth; bring to a boil and stir in soy sauce mixture. Cook until thickened, stirring occasionally, about 2 minutes.

4) Remove from heat; add 1/4 cup cashews and gently mix to combine.

5) Serve ladled over a bed of rice garnished with remaining cashews.

Makes 4 servings

# Chicken Marsala

**4 boneless chicken breasts**

**1/4 cup all-purpose flour**
**1/2 teaspoon salt**
**1/4 tablespoon ground black pepper**
**1/2 teaspoon dried oregano**
**2 tablespoons olive oil**
**2 tablespoons butter**
**1 cup sliced fresh mushrooms**
**2/3 cup (sweet) Marsala wine**
**1/4 cup white cooking sherry**

1)  With kitchen mallet, pound chicken breasts until flat and thin. Set aside.

2)  In a shallow dish mix together flour, salt, pepper and oregano. Dredge chicken in flour mixture.

3)  Heat oil and butter in a large skillet until hot; cook chicken in batches until golden browned on each side, about 2 minutes per side. Transfer to serving platter and keep warm.

4)  Add mushrooms to same skillet and cook for 2 minutes, stirring. Add wine and sherry, stirring up browned bits, and reduce volume by half. Pour sauce of chicken cutlets and serve.

## Makes 4 servings

# Chicken with Orange Peel Stir Fry

**1 2-pound fryer or 2 chicken breasts, boned and skinned, cut into
1-inch pieces
1/4 teaspoon salt
2 tablespoons dark soy sauce
1 tablespoon cornstarch
4 cups oil for deep frying
2 tablespoons sesame seed oil
2 tablespoons preserved orange peel or fresh dried orange rind,\* cut
into chunks
1 tablespoon scallion, chopped fine
1 tablespoon ginger, chopped fine
2 whole dried red chili peppers, cut into quarters
4 1/2 teaspoons sherry
1 teaspoon red wine vinegar
3/4 tablespoon sugar**

1) Sprinkle chicken with salt. Mix with 1 tablespoon of soy sauce and cornstarch.

2) Heat oil to boiling in wok. Deep fry chicken 1 minute. Drain. Remove chicken and oil.

3) Heat sesame oil in wok. Stir fry orange peel, scallion, ginger, and chili peppers 1 minute. Add sherry, 1 tablespoon soy sauce, wine vinegar, and sugar. Then add chicken. Stir fry 2 minutes. Remove to platter. Serve hot.

Serves 4 to 6

# Chicken in Wine Sauce

**1 chicken, cut up**

**2 tablespoons olive oil**
**1 medium onion, chopped**
**3/4 cup dry red wine**
**1/4 cup cider vinegar**
**1 tablespoon Worcestershire sauce**
**1 teaspoon salt**
**2 large cloves garlic, minced**
**1/2 teaspoon ground coriander**
**1/2 teaspoon cayenne pepper**
**1/2 teaspoon ground cumin**
**1 large green or red bell pepper, chopped**
**12 pitted prunes, halved**
**12 pimento-stuffed olives**
**1/4 cup tomato paste**
**2 tablespoons capers**
**Steamed rice**

1)  Rinse the chicken pieces and pat them dry. In a large skillet over medium-high heat, brown the chicken on all sides for about 15 minutes. Remove the chicken and add the onion to the drippings. Fry till tender and golden. Drain off excess fat. Return chicken to the pan along with the liquids and all of the spices. Simmer for 25 minutes.

2)  Stir in the green pepper, the prunes, olives, tomato paste and capers. Cook and simmer 20 more minutes or until chicken is fork tender. Skim off fat. Transfer chicken and all sauce to a serving platter. Pass the steamed rice around with it.

Serves 4

# Southwest Chicken Skillet

**2 tablespoons vegetable oil**

**6 chicken breast halves**
**Salt and freshly ground black pepper to taste**
**6 garlic cloves, finely chopped**
**1 (14 1/2-ounce) can Mexican-style stewed tomatoes**
**1 large yam, peeled, cut into 1/2-inch dice**
**1 (4-ounce) can diced green chilies**
**1 (15-ounce can)yellow or white hominy, drained**
**1/2 cup chicken broth**
**1/2 cup packed chopped fresh cilantro, divided**
**1/4 cup bottled mild green taco sauce**

1) Heat oil in large skillet over medium-high heat. Season chicken with salt and pepper. Sauté chicken until golden brown, about 4 minutes per side. Transfer chicken to a bowl; set aside.

2) Pour off all but 1 tablespoon drippings from skillet. Add garlic and cook about 30 seconds. Add stewed tomatoes, yam, chilies, hominy, broth, 1/4 cup cilantro and taco sauce.

3) Return chicken to skillet, including any juices in bowl, stir to combine and cover skillet. Reduce heat to medium-low and simmer until chicken is just tender, about 20 minutes, removing cover last 5 minutes to reduce juices to sauce consistency.

4) Transfer to large deep serving platter. Garnish with remaining cilantro.

## Serves 4 to 6

# Baked Fish Fillets

**1 pound fresh or frozen fillets**
**1 tablespoon lemon juice**
**1/8 teaspoon paprika**
**Salt and freshly ground black pepper to taste**
**1 tablespoon butter or margarine**
**1 tablespoon all-purpose flour**
**1/2 cup milk**
**1/4 cup buttered bread crumbs**
**1 tablespoon snipped parsley for garnish**

1) Thaw frozen fillets; cut into serving-size pieces. Place in a greased shallow baking dish. Sprinkle with lemon juice, paprika, salt and pepper.

2) In saucepan, melt butter; blend in flour and cook 30 seconds. Stir in milk; cook and stir until thickened and bubbly; season with salt and pepper. Pour sauce over fillets. Sprinkle with crumbs.

3) Bake, uncovered, at 350*F (175*C) for 35 minutes or until fish flakes easily. Garnish with parsley, if desired.

Serves 2 to 4

# Skillet Orange Roughy

**1 tablespoon butter**
**1 1/2 pounds orange roughy fillets, about 1/2-inch thick**
**2 tablespoons fresh lemon juice**
**Salt and freshly ground black pepper to taste**
**2 tablespoons chopped flat-leaf parsley**
**1 lemon, cut into wedges**

1) Melt butter in a heavy nonstick skillet over medium heat. Arrange fillets in skillet. Drizzle with lemon juice and season with salt and pepper.

2) Cover skillet and simmer 8 to 10 minutes or until fish flakes easily.

3) Serve with parsley and lemon wedges.

Makes 4 servings

# Tuna Steaks with Pasta and Tomato Sauce

**2 tablespoons butter**
**2 tablespoons olive oil**
**1 green bell pepper, seeded, chopped**
**2 garlic cloves, finely minced**
**1 1/2 drained canned diced tomatoes**
**1/2 cup bottled clam juice**
**1/3 cup chopped fresh cilantro**
**1/2 cup dry white wine**
**1/4 cup water**
**3 tablespoons fresh lemon juice**
**Salt and freshly ground pepper to taste**
**1/4 teaspoon crushed dried red pepper**
**1/2 cup all purpose flour**
**1/2 teaspoon garlic powder**
**4 6 to 8-ounce tuna steaks**
**12 ounces angel hair pasta, cooked according to package**
**1/4 cup freshly grated Parmesan cheese for garnish**
**Chopped fresh cilantro for garnish**

1) Melt 1 tablespoon butter with 1 tablespoon oil in heavy large skillet over medium-high heat. Add bell pepper and minced garlic; cook until peppers are almost tender, about 5 minutes.

2) Add tomatoes, clam juice, 1/3 cup cilantro, wine, water, lemon juice and dried red pepper. Bring to boil. Reduce heat; simmer until flavors blend, about 5 minutes. Season with salt and pepper.

3) Mix flour and garlic powder in shallow bowl. Season tuna with salt and pepper. Coat with flour mixture, shaking off excess.

4) Melt remaining 1 tablespoon butter with 1 tablespoon oil in another large skillet over high heat. Add tuna to skillet and cook about 2 to 3 minutes per side.

5) Bring sauce to simmer over medium heat. Add tuna; cook for 2 to 3 minutes, or until desired doneness.

6) Place tuna steaks on pasta and spoon sauce over. Sprinkle with Parmesan and cilantro and serve.

Serves 4

# Nantucket Clam Chowder

In New England all hard-shell clams are called by the Pequot Indian name, quahog. Quahogs can be littlenecks, cherrystones, or the fully mature "chowder clam" (used for chowders and stuffings because they're deemed too tough for anything else.)

**1/4 pound salt pork or slab bacon, finely diced**
**1 quart quahogs, packed in 1 cup liquid**
**2 cups water**
**1 large yellow onion, finely diced**
**1/2 cup pounded common crackers***
**2 1/2 cups diced new potatoes**
**4 cups milk or half-n-half**
**8 teaspoons unsalted butter**
**Salt and freshly ground black pepper**

1) In a large, heavy-bottomed saucepan or a stockpot over medium-high heat, sautè the pork fat or bacon until as much fat as possible is rendered and all that remains solid are the cracklings. Remove the cracklings and reserve. Remove all but 2 tablespoons of the fat.

2) Take the quahogs out of their liquid and reserve the liquid. Rinse them in the 2 cups water. Strain the water and reserve. Finely mince the quahogs.

3) Sauté the onion and quahogs together in the pork fat for about 5 minutes. Combine the pounded biscuit with the clam sauté. Add the quahog liquid and the reserved rinse water. Add the potatoes and cook until tender, 10 to 15 minutes. Add the cracklings. In a saucepan, heat the milk or half-n-half; do not boil. Add to the chowder.

4) Serve hot with a teaspoon of unsalted butter in each bowl and salt and freshly ground pepper to taste.

## Serves 8.

*To break up the crackers, wrap them in a kitchen towel and pound with a wooden or rubber mallet.

Variation: To thicken the chowder without using wheat, prepare 1 cup potato puree and add to the chowder instead of the biscuits. Use 2 cups rather than 2 1/2 cups diced new potatoes.

# Old-Fashioned Beef Stew

**2 tablespoon all-purpose flour**
**1 pound beef or pork stew meat, cut into 3/4-inch cubes**
**2 tablespoons vegetable oil**
**3 1/2 cups tomato-vegetable juice**
**1 medium onion, cut into thin wedges**
**2 teaspoons beef base or instant bouillon granules**
**2 teaspoons Worcestershire sauce**
**1 bay leaf**
**1 1/2 teaspoons snipped fresh marjoram or 1/2 teaspoon dried marjoram, crushed**
**1 1/2 teaspoon snipped fresh oregano to 1/2 teaspoon dried oregano, crushed**
**1 teaspoon salt**
**1/4 teaspoon pepper**
**2 1/2 cups cubed potatoes**
**1 cup frozen cut green beans**
**1 cup frozen whole kernel corn**
**1 cup sliced carrots**

1) Place flour in a plastic or paper bag. Add meat cubes, a few at a time, shaking to coat.

2) In a Dutch oven, brown meat, half at a time, in hot oil. Drain fat.

3) Stir in vegetable juice, onion, beef base or granules, Worcestershire sauce, bay leaf, marjoram, oregano, salt and pepper. Bring to boiling; reduce heat. Cover and simmer for 1 to 1/12 hours for beef (about 30 minutes for pork) or until meat is nearly tender.

4) Stir in potatoes, green beans, corn and carrots. Return to boiling; reduce heat. Cover and simmer about 30 minute more or until meat and vegetables are tender. Discard bay leaf.

Makes 4 servings.

**Crock-Pot Directions:** Prepare and brown meat as above. In a 3 1/3 to 4-quart crock pot or slow cooker, layer meat, onion, potatoes, green beans, corn and carrots. Decrease vegetable juice to 2 1/2 cups. Combine the vegetable juice, beef base or granules, Worcestershire, bay leaf, marjoram, oregano, salt and pepper. Pour over vegetables. Cover and cook on low-heat for 10 to 12 hours or until meat and vegetables are tender.

# Beef and Barley Soup

**2 pounds lean ground beef**

**2 tablespoons vegetable or olive oil**
**2 cups diced carrots**
**2 cups diced onion**
**2 cups diced celery**
**2 cloves garlic, minced**
**3 cups cooked barley**
**8 cups beef broth**
**2 (14 to16-ounce) cans Italian-style stewed tomatoes**
**1/2 cup dry red wine**
**1 teaspoon dried thyme**
**Salt and pepper to taste**
**1/4 cup minced fresh parsley**
**Balsamic vinegar (optional)**

1)  In a large pot or Dutch oven, cook ground beef on medium-high heat until browned, breaking up with a spatula or fork as it cooks. Remove beef from pan and set aside.

2)  Add oil to pan; add carrots, onion, celery and garlic; cook until vegetables are tender, about 5 minutes, stirring occasionally.

3)  Return beef and all remaining ingredients, except parsley and optional vinegar. Bring to boil on high heat; reduce heat to a simmer, cover. Simmer 20 minutes.

4)  Stir in parsley and taste. Adjust seasoning, adding more salt or pepper if needed, or a splash of balsamic vinegar if soup needs a little more zip.

Makes 8 servings

# Greek Chicken-Lemon Soup

When Greek cooks want a quick, refreshing lunch, they put a pot of chicken broth on the stove to transform into their beloved pastel yellow, citrus-scented soup called avgolemono. This rendition is accented with a sprinkle of fresh dill; the soup would lose its delicacy with dried dill, so if you don't have fresh, simply omit it.

**6 cups Basic Chicken Soup or canned low-sodium chicken broth**
**1/2 cup long-grain rice**
**1/2 pound skinless, boneless chicken breasts, cut into 1/2-inch cubes**
**2 large eggs, at room temperature**
**1/4 cup fresh lemon juice**
**1 tablespoon minced fresh dill**

1) In a large nonreactive saucepan or Dutch oven, bring the broth to a boil over medium-high heat. Gradually stir in the rice, keeping the broth at a boil, and reduce the heat to medium-low. Simmer, partially covered, until the rice is cooked through, 5 to 7 minutes. Remove the pot from the heat.

2) In a small bowl, whisk the eggs to blend. Gradually beat in the lemon juice. Slowly whisk about 1 cup of the hot soup into the eggs. Stirring constantly, gradually pour the egg mixture into the soup. Return the pot to the stove and cook over low heat, stirring constantly, just until the soup is thickened slightly, about 1 minute. Do not let the liquid come to a simmer, or the eggs will curdle. Stir in the dill. Serve at once. (Reheat any leftover soup in the top part of a double boiler over simmering water.)

Makes 6 to 8 servings

# Hearty Vegetable Soup

**3 tablespoons olive oil**
**3 large carrots, peeled, coarsely chopped**
**1/2 large head green cabbage, thinly sliced**
**1 onion, chopped**
**2 celery stalks, chopped**
**2 tablespoons chopped fresh rosemary or 1 tablespoon dried**
**6 cups vegetable or chicken broth**
**1 (28-ounce) can ready-cut tomatoes with juice**
**1/3 cup freshly grated Parmesan cheese**
**Additional freshly grated Parmesan cheese**

1) Heat olive oil in Dutch oven over medium heat. Add carrots, cabbage, onion, celery and rosemary. Saute until tender and beginning to brown, about 10 minutes. Add broth and tomatoes with juice; simmer for 45 minutes. Season soup to taste with salt and pepper.

2) Stir in 1/3 cup Parmesan. Ladle soup into bowls. Serve, passing additional cheese separately.

## Serves 8

# Apricots and Wild Rice

Wild rice is actually the nutty-flavored seed of a long-grain marsh grass. It's expensive, and so is often used in combination with grains like the pearl barley in this recipe.

**3/4 cup wild rice, uncooked**
**3 cups chicken broth**
**1/2 cup pearl barley, uncooked**
**1/2 cup chopped dried apricots**
**1/4 cup currants**
**1 tablespoon butter or margarine**
**1/3 cup sliced almonds, toasted**

1) Combine wild rice and chicken broth in a medium saucepan. Bring to a boil; cover, reduce heat, and simmer 10 minutes. Remove from heat; stir in barley, apricots, currants, and butter.

2) Pour mixture into an ungreased 1 1/2-quart casserole. Cover and bake at 325*F (160*C) for 30 minutes or until rice and barley are tender and liquid is absorbed. Gently stir in almonds.

Makes 6 servings

# Parmesan Garlic Potatoes

**6 tablespoons butter, melted**
**1/2 teaspoon garlic powder**
**3 tablespoons freshly grated Parmesan cheese**
**8 medium unpeeled red potatoes, washed and halved lengthwise**

1) Preheat oven to 375*F (190*C).

2) Pour butter into a 13 x 9 x 2-inch baking pan. Sprinkle garlic powder and Parmesan cheese over butter. Place potatoes with cut side down over cheese mixture.

3) Bake, uncovered for 40 to 45 minutes or until tender.

Serves 6 to 8

# Sweet Potato Apple Dish

**1 (28-ounce) can sweet potatoes, drained and cut up**
**1(21-ounce) can apple pie filling**
**1/2 teaspoon ground cinnamon**
**1/2 cup chopped walnuts**
**1/2 cup shredded coconut**
**1/4 cup butter, melted**
**2 cups miniature marshmallows**

1) Preheat oven to 350*F (175*C).

2) Combine sweet potatoes, pie filling and cinnamon and pour into a greased, 13 x 9 x 2-inch baking dish. Sprinkle nuts and coconut evenly over top and drizzle with butter.

3) Bake for 20 minutes; top with marshmallows and bake for another 5 minutes or until marshmallows are toasted golden brown.

Serves 8

# Raspberry Sweet Potatoes

**8 medium-size sweet potatoes**
**1 teaspoon salt**
**1/4 cup firmly packed brown sugar**
**1/4 cup butter or margarine, softened**
**1 (10-ounce) package frozen raspberries, thawed and undrained**

1) Cook sweet potatoes in boiling salted water 20 to 25 minutes or until tender. Drain and let cool to touch. Peel and cut in half lengthwise.

2) Arrange sweet potatoes in a lightly greased 13 x 9 x 2-inch casserole, cut side up.

3) Combine brown sugar and butter in a small bowl, mixing well.

4) Spread brown sugar mixture over cut surface of sweet potatoes. Top with raspberries and juice.

5) Bake uncovered, at 350*F (175*C). for 25 minutes, spooning raspberries and juice over potatoes occasionally.

Makes 8 to 10 servings

# Marinated Grilled Portobella Mushrooms

This recipe is a favorite of those who like marinated mushrooms.

Remember, however, that portabellas act like sponges, so marinate the mushrooms for only a short period of time, or the resulting dish will be very vinegary and unpleasant.

**4 large Portobella caps, 4 to 6 inches in diameter**
**1 cup extra virgin olive oil**
**1 cup red or white wine vinegar**
**2 tablespoons soy sauce**
**1 tablespoon sugar**
**1 tablespoon dried herbs or 1/2 cup finely chopped fresh herbs**

1) Remove the stems from the caps of the mushrooms. Save for use in another recipe, if desired.

2) Combine the remaining of ingredients and blend well with a whisk. Let the marinade sit for 1 hour until the herbs soften.

3) Prepare the grill.

4) Place the mushrooms in a shallow non-metallic dish or pan and pour the marinade over the mushrooms. Let the mushrooms marinate for 10 minutes, turning occasionally to ensure uniform coating. Remove the mushrooms from the marinade and place on the hot grill. Grill on each side for 2 to 3 minutes. Remove from the grill, slice, and serve immediately.

Note: If you don't have a grill, you can bake the portabellas in a 350*F (175*C) oven for 5 to 7 minutes.

Serves 4

# Baby Carrots with Gran Marnier

**1 pound of baby whole carrots**
**1/2 cup Gran Marnier**
**1/4 cup butter**
**Salt and freshly ground black pepper to taste**
**1 tablespoon chopped fresh parsley (optional)**

1) Cook carrots in a large skillet, covered, in a small amount of water over medium heat until almost tender. Drain.

2) Add the butter and Gran Marnier and heat slowly, stirring until liquid is reduced by half and carrots have absorbed the flavor.

3) Season with salt and pepper. Sprinkle with parsley, if desired and serve.

## Makes 4 to 6 servings.

# Layered Tuna and Pasta Salad

Serve this delicious salad in a glass bowl with straight sides to display all the colorful layers.

**1 1/3 cups dry cavatelli or medium shell macaroni**
**4 cups shredded iceberg lettuce**
**1 cup chopped, seeded cucumber**
**1 cup chopped, seeded tomato**
**1 (9 1/2-ounce) can chunk white tuna, drained and broken into chunks**
**1 cup frozen peas**
**1 (2 1/2-ounce) can sliced ripe olives, drained**
**2 hard-cooked eggs, sliced**
**Herb Dressing (recipe follows)**
**1/2 cup finely shredded cheddar or Monterey Jack cheese**
**2 tablespoons sliced green onion**

1) Cook pasta according to package directions, preferably al dente (firm to the bite). Drain; rinse with cold water and drain again.

2) Place shredded lettuce in the bottom of a 3-quart glass salad bowl with straight sides or other similar serving dish.

3) Layer the remaining ingredients in the following order: Cooked pasta, cucumber, tomato, tuna, peas, olives, and egg slices.

4) Carefully spread the Herb Dressing evenly over top of salad, sealing to the edge of the bowl. Sprinkle with the cheese and green onion.

5) Cover tightly with plastic wrap. Chill salad for 4 hours or overnight.

6) To serve, toss layers lightly to mix.

Makes 6 servings

## Herb Dressing
**1/2 cup mayonnaise or salad dressing**
**1/3 cup plain yogurt**
**1/4 cup chopped flat-leaf parsley (Italian parsley)**
**1 tablespoon snipped fresh chives**
**1 tablespoon fresh lemon juice**
**1 tablespoon Dijon mustard**
**Freshly ground pepper to taste**

1) Combine all ingredients in a small bowl, mixing well. Makes 1 cup.

# Chicken Pecan Salad

**6 ounces chicken breast, boiled or baked**
**1 cup celery, diced**
**4 apples**
**1 cup pecans, chopped**
**1/2 cup fat free mayonnaise**
**1/2 cup sour cream, reduced fat**

Mix mayonnaise and sour cream. Combine ingredients, add pecans just prior to serving. Hollow out avocado and serve salad inside; or serve on bed of lettuce and garnish with avocado. Yields 4 servings.

## PECAN-CRUSTED TROUT

A crunchy coating for an American favorite gives this fresh trout special appeal. Add boiled new potatoes or rice pilaf and a green vegetable for a tasty dinner.

**4 large trout fillets (about 6-8 ounces each)**
**Salt & pepper to taste**
**Fresh lemon juice to taste**
**1/2 cup seasoned bread crumbs, divided in half**
**1 cup roasted pecans (5-7 minutes at 350 degrees, until deep brown and glossy)**
**2 teaspoons rosemary**
**1/3 cup all-purpose flour**
**1 egg beaten with 2-3 teaspoons water**
**2 tablespoon vegetable oil, divided in half**
**2 tablespoon butter, divided in half**

Season trout fillets with salt, pepper and lemon juice. Let stand at room temperature for 10 to 15 minutes. Combine 2 tablespoons of bread crumbs with pecans in blender or food processor. Grind pecans finely, combine with remaining bread crumbs and rosemary and transfer to plate. Dredge fillets in flour, shake off excess. Dip in egg wash. Place fillets skin-side up on crumb mixture, pressing into flesh. In large skillet heat 1 tablespoon each of oil and butter over medium-high heat. Place 2 fillets, skin-side up in skillet and cook until golden brown, about 3 minutes. Using spatula, turn fillets and cook until opaque in center, about 3 more minutes. Transfer to plate. Repeat with remaining butter, oil and fillets. Yields 4 main dish servings.

**Recipes courtesy of the Georgia Pecan Commission at www.georgiapecans.com**

# Grandma Me's Chop Suey

Alicia Schilling


This was one of my favorite recipes when I was growing up. We'd often eat dinner at my Grandma Me's (my little sister was named Alicia after my grandma and my sister dubbed her "Grandma Me".

**1 lb Chuck Roast**
**1 lb Pork Roast**
**2 large cans LaChoy Chinese Vegetables**
**2 large cans or 1 lb fresh bean sprouts**
**2 large cans crispy Chow Mein noodles**
**2 large cans of water chestnuts**
**2 large cans or 1 lb fresh mushrooms**
**2 cups chopped celery**
**1 large onion**
**Soy Sauce**
**Cornstarch**
Water
2 tbsp. Oriental brown gravy sauce

In large stock pot or pan, brown and cook beef and pork in small amount of oil. Remove meat from pan, leaving drippings, and cut away fat and bone. Cut meat into small cubes. Put back into pan and sauté chopped onion and celery. Add drained sprouts, Chinese vegetables, water chestnuts and mushrooms to pan. Add enough water as needed to make a broth and add gravy sauce. Make a thickening with 2 tbsp of cornstarch and water.Stir into Chop Suey mixture and stir over medium heat until thickened. Serve over chowmein noodles or rice. Add soy sauce for flavor.

# Macaroni with Bacon and Tomato

DeEtta Koning

This was favorite recipe my mom would fix when we needed a quick, yummy dinner.

**2 Cups macaroni**
**1 Medium onion (diced)**
**½ lb. Bacon**
**28 oz. Can of Tomato Juice or Stewed Tomatos**

Prepare macaroni as directed. Slice bacon into strips and fry in skillet. When crisp, add diced onions and sauté. Add to drained macaroni and add tomato juice. Let this simmer for about 10 minutes. Season with salt and pepper to taste.

# Grandma Me's Scalloped Potatoes

Alicia Schilling

**1 can cream of mushroom soup**
**¾ cup milk**
**dash of pepper**
**4 cups sliced potatoes**
**1 Tblsp butter or margarine**
**dash of paprika**

Blend soup, milk and pepper. Set aside. Alternate layers of potatoes, onion and sauce in 1-1/2 quart dish. Dot with butter. Cover and bake at 375 degrees for one hour. Uncover and bake for 15 additional minutes.  You can also add diced ham as a layer.

# Spanish Style Pork Chops

DeEtta Koning
Another quick recipe my mom would make.

**Package of 6 or 9 thinly cut pork chops**
**1 package of beef flavored instant rice**
**1 can of stewed or diced tomatoes**

Brown chops on both sides and remove from skillet. Cook rice according to directions. Add tomatoes. When rice is tender, turn heat to simmer, add pork chops and cover. Simmer for 30-45 minutes.

Variation: Use Spanish-style instant rice or Mexican-flavored diced tomatoes. You can also add a ¼-tsp of cumin and some fresh chopped cilantro.

# Chicken Broccoli Casserole

Norma Heater

This recipe comes from one of my mom's former beauty shop customers and a great friend of our family.

**4 Cups cooked chicken, chopped**
**2 10-oz packages frozen broccoli**
**½ -cup mayonnaise or salad dressing**
**2 tsp lemon juice**
**2 Cans cream of chicken soup**
**½ tsp curry powder**
**½ package herbed stuffing mix**
**½-cup melted margarine (or chicken broth)**
**Parmesan Cheese**

Mix stuffing mix with margarine or broth. Add ½ of stuffing mixture to greased 9x13 casserole dish or pan. Reserving ½ can of soup, add remaining ingredients to the other half of stuffing mix and combine well. Put into casserole dish and top with reserved soup and sprinkle with parmesan cheese and remaining stuffing mixture. Dot with butter if desired. Bake at 350 degrees for 35-40 minutes.

# Roy's Emergency Squad 51 Firehouse Chili

Brian Koning

My younger sister had an imaginary friend when she was younger. He was "Roy" from the 1970s television show, "Emergency". This is my own chili recipe that I named in honor of Alicia's little invisible paramedic pal. (She's now a Registered Nurse…what a coincidence!)

**Large jar of spaghetti sauce**
**Medium Onion**
**Three chili peppers**
**1 lb hamburger or ground chuck**
**1 lb smoke sausage (skinned and diced small)**
**2 cans of warm beer**
**1 large can of kidney beans**
**Chili powder**
**Texas style hot pepper sauce**
**¼ cup of chocolate syrup**
**Macaroni (optional)**

In large stockpot, brown beef and sausage with onion and two diced and seeded chili peppers. Add dash of chili powder and dash of hot pepper sauce. Drain grease from meat. Add spaghetti sauce, beer, beans, chocolate and one chili pepper (halved). Bring to a boil and then let simmer for at least one hour. If you add macaroni, add it 30 minutes prior to serving or cook in advance and serve on the side for people who want to add it. You can also put bowls of grated cheddar or American cheese, oyster crackers and onions.

# Zucchini Casserole

DeEtta Koning

Layer in this order in a 1-1/2 quart dish.

**Sliced Zucchini**
**Sliced Onions**
**Cracker Crumbs**
**Sliced tomatoes**
**Velveeta cheese slices**
**Ground Sausage, browned and crumbled**
**2 cans cream of mushroom soup**

Bake at 350 degrees for 1 hour.

# Grandma Koning's Honey Glazed Carrots

Lora E. Koning
My Grandma Koning was one of my cooking mentors. Whenever I had a question, I could call her and she would give me directions or the recipe right over the telephone.

16 peeled carrots and sliced one lengthwise and cut into 1-inch sections. Put carrots into lightly buttered casserole dish and add ½ cup boiling water and 1 tsp salt. Bake at 400 degrees until carrots are tender (about 45 minutes). Drain and drizzle mixture of 2 tblsp butter, ¼ cup honey, ½ tblsp lemon juice over carrots and bake for five more minutes.

# Get your **FREE...**

## *E-mail newsletter, special offers, updates and more when you...*

## **Register Online!**

Register online at www.personalchefmarketing.com and you'll get a FREE subscription to my E-mail newsletter, PC Marketing. I'll provide tips, tricks and tactics for marketing your personal chef business including press releases, television appearances, prospecting, selling and more, . You'll also find out about special offers on cookware, spices, cutlery, clothing and other great offerings.

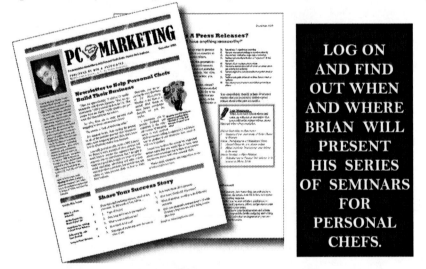

LOG ON
AND FIND
OUT WHEN
AND WHERE
BRIAN WILL
PRESENT
HIS SERIES
OF SEMINARS
FOR
PERSONAL
CHEFS.

**No registration fees. No hidden costs. Just visit this Web page and enter the requested information:**

# **www.personalchefmarketing.com**

**PERSONAL CHEF**
*Marketing*
*Recipes for Success.*

120-21-962-LHH

# BRIAN KONING

Born and raised in Lafayette, Indiana, Brian Koning was fortunate to have been able to develop cooking skills from his parents as well as both of his maternal and paternal grandparents who lived just blocks away.

His musical and singing talents earned him a full scholarship to Purdue University where he was a baritone soloist with the Purdue University Varsity Glee Club. Because the group travelled extensively, Brian was exposed to a wide variety of regional and ethnic cuisine which intensified his passion for cooking.

After graduating in 1986, he worked in a variety of marketing, advertising and sales positions as well as launching several small business ventures. He also toured with his own band for six years as lead singer and guitarist. In 1998, he retired from the entertainment industry trading the stage and late nights for a corporate cubicle and a stable day job. A marketing job offer initiated a move to Indianapolis in 1999.

In 2000, Brian's position as Director of Markeing was eliminated when the venture funded dot com company he was working for missed it's critical round of funding and collapsed. A friend introduced him to the personal chef industry. He saw an opportunity to combine his love for cooking with his marketing, sales and business skills. He started Doctor Dinner Personal Chef Service in February of 2001.

Today, Brian still cooks for several clients and offers marketing support and guidance to new and struggling personal chefs. He is also a marketing consultant for a select group of companies. He continues his love for performing by frequently appearing in plays and musical theater productions. He has been married to wife, Doreen, since 1985 and has two daughters, Kaitlin and Karli, and one son, Kyler.

Printed in the United States
29388LVS00005B/87

9 781418 408954